OPPORTUNITIES IN
TRAVEL CAREERS

Robert Scott Milne

Foreword by
William S. Norman
President & CEO
Travel Industry Association of America

VGM Career Horizons
NTC/Contemporary Publishing Group

Library of Congress Cataloging-in-Publication Data

Milne, Robert Scott.
    Opportunities in travel careers / Robert Scott Milne ; foreword
by William S. Norman.
       p.   cm.—(VGM Opportunities series)
    Includes bibliographical references.
    ISBN 0-8442-4639-5 (hardcover).—ISBN 0-8442-4640-9
(paperback)
    1. Tourist trade—Vocational guidance.   I. Title.   II. Series.
G155.5.M55   1996
338.4′791′02373—dc20
                                       96-1242
                                       CIP

Cover Photo Credits:
Upper left and lower right courtesy of Amtrak; upper right and lower left courtesy
of United Airlines.

Published by VGM Career Horizons
An imprint of NTC/Contemporary Publishing Company
4255 West Touhy Avenue, Lincolnwood (Chicago), Illinois 60646-1975 U.S.A.
Copyright © 1996 by NTC/Contemporary Publishing Company
Printed in the United States of America
International Standard Book Number: 0-8442-4639-5 (cloth)
                                      0-8442-4640-9 (paper)

18   17   16   15   14   13   12   11   10   9   8   7   6   5   4   3   2

CONTENTS

Origin and development of travel. Tourism. Growth
and stability in this field. Perks in the travel industry.
Opportunities for women. The broad variety of travel
jobs.

Flight attendants. Pilots and copilots. Flight
engineers. Aircraft mechanics. Ticket agents,
reservation agents, and clerks. Air traffic controllers.
Aviation safety inspectors.

Job opportunities. Wage scales.

ABOUT THE AUTHOR

Robert Scott Milne has been a full-time freelance travel writer since 1972. Before that he was an encyclopedia editor for sixteen years, first at *Collier's Encyclopedia* and then at *Encyclopedia Americana;* he was also moonlighting during those years—writing travel articles for various publications. He became an active member of the Society of American Travel Writers in 1966. The society's Freelance Council has given him a special award for the monthly newsletter he edits and publishes, *Travelwriter Marketletter,* which gives valuable marketing leads to travel writers and photographers, and information on trips being offered to them. He is a founding member of the Travel Journalists Guild and was secretary of the Council of Writers Organizations, comprised of over 23,000 members. He is also a member of the International Food, Wine & Travel Writers Association, the Authors Guild, the American Society of Journalists & Authors, Media Alliance, the New York Travel Writers' Association, the Society of Professional Journalists, Naval Intelligence Professionals, and the Newsletter Publishers Association.

Among the periodicals that have published his travel articles are: the *New York Times, New York Post,* and *New York News, Chicago Tribune,* and numerous other newspapers; *Modern Bride, Atlantic Monthly, Seventeen, Cruise Travel, Popular Mechanics, Travel Holiday, Travel Agent Magazine, Writer's Digest,* and many other magazines. He has also written for Exxon, Texaco, and other travel guides. He has written thousands of articles for the two encyclopedias previously mentioned, and for many other encyclopedias and yearbooks. Among the books to which he has contributed are *The Complete Guide to Writing Nonfiction, Around the World with the Experts, The Great Escape,* and *Mrs. Siu's Chinese Cookbook.*

From 1972 through 1989 he maintained his own office—the envy of the travel-writing world—in the Plaza Hotel in New York City, then moved to the Waldorf-Astoria. With his Vienna-born wife, Gaby, who is a musician, he lives in Elmsford, New York. They share the house with two dogs and a parrot, Canaima, purchased from Indians in a Venezuela jungle camp. The Milnes travel extensively.

ACKNOWLEDGMENTS

Canadian travel-career information was added in the second, third, and fourth editions, and expanded in this fifth edition. The author's special thanks go to the many Canadians mentioned below for their eagerly proffered aid. This book would not have been possible without the wholehearted cooperation of many people in all facets of the travel industry. For information, pictures, statements about the future of the industry, and many other kinds of assistance, the author sincerely thanks the following people: Eunice Juckett Meeker, freelance travel writer; Christine Maddox, editor; Janet Luoma; Marie Thérèse Deprez; Harry Mullikin, former president of Westin Hotels, Regina Henry of Westin's New York office, and Ron LaRue of the Seattle headquarters; Marguerite Allen, senior vice president, Robert Warner Distinguished Hotels; William D. Toohey and Edward R. Book, past presidents, and Edward S. Norman, president, Travel Industry Association of America (TIA); J. A. Carman, Dawna Kluver, Bruce Paton, Sam McKelvey, and Diana Rayner of the Canadian Government Office of Tourism; Janet R. Hafner of the Canadian Government Information Service Library in New York; Dr. Heinz Patzak, Paris Representative, Austrian National Tourist Office; Jason King, president of Yours in Travel Personnel Agency in New York; Dr. Samuel I. Porrath, founder and chairman of the Transportation, Travel, and Tourism Institute (TTT) at Niagara University; Robert

Lonati, Secretary-General of the World Tourism Organization, headquartered in Madrid; Kathy M. Burns of Monterey Peninsula College; Albert E. Kudrle, formerly of the American Hotel & Motel Association and now a public relations consultant; Professor James M. Rovelstad; Richard J. Sullivan of Notre Dame; Irving W. Morrill, coordinator of the TTT Program at Adelphi University; David H. Lobb; Arthur W. Jackson of American Airlines; Alan B. Wayne; Charles Novak of United Airlines; Harriette S. Parker; Jay Beau-Seigneur; Jeff Kreindler and James A. Arey; Robert Randell; Walter Menke of Trans World Airlines; Bunny Obermeyer, former senior flight attendant on TWA; the late Eugene Du Bois; Gil Perlroth; Steve Pisni; Edward Wojtas of Amtrak; Patrick R. Sheridan, president of Gray Line Sight-Seeing Companies; Gene Teeling and Kathy McFadden of Greyhound Lines; Kim M. Arnone of Continental Trailways; James J. Sheeran, president of Creative Marketing Management in New York; Daniel Z. Henkin, vice president of the Air Transport Association; Patricia Rose and Sheridan H. Garth of Thomas Cook & Son; Monica Burke of Inter-Continental Hotels; public relations specialist Linda Kundell in New York; Edwina Arnold of Club Méditerranée; Hella Rothwell of Hella M. Rothwell PR in New York; Philip D. Shea and Al Banks of The Sheraton Corporation; James L. Shanahan; Jacques C. Cossé of Jacques C. Cossé and Associates in Beverly Hills; Philip Miles of Loews Hotels; Lis K. Brewer of Hilton International; Karen Escalera of Karen Weiner Escalera Associates in New York; the late John W. Hill, founder of Hill & Knowlton; Jafar Jafari, editor of *Annals of Tourism Research* at the University of Wisconsin–Stout, in Menomonie, Wisconsin; Debbie Swanson; Donald Reynolds, Leslie Stackel, and Barbara Wright of the American Society of Travel Agents (ASTA); Robert Jackson of the United States Travel Service in the Department of Commerce; Ida Singleton of the U.S. Office of Personnel Management; Vance H. Anthony and Connolly Hall

Dillon of the U.S. Bureau of Labor Statistics; Alan Bell, PR practitioner in New York; Redmond Tyler and Gail Shore; Barbara Taylor of Alden Taylor & Associates; Lois Tilles of the Institute of Certified Travel Agents; Richard Feldman and Emilie A. MacLachlan of the Public Relations Society of America; Georgia Beach, director of public relations for Hyatt International; M. Jane Turner of TWA; Jackie B. Pate of Delta Airlines; Shirley Stern of the American Hotel & Motel Association; William E. Stephan, president of the Membership of Independent Travel Agents; Barbara Stoltz of the Travel Education Center; Don Henkel of the National Recreation and Parks Association; my patient and perceptive editors at National Textbook Company, Barbara Wood Donner, Betsy Lancefield, Ellen Urban, and Michael K. Urban; and for much forbearance while I wrote the first, second, third, fourth, and fifth editions of this book, my wife Gaby.

FOREWORD

Profound fundamental structural changes in the U.S. economy—which have gone largely unnoticed—have escalated the importance of the travel and tourism industry to the nation's well-being. The travel industry's meteoric rise to become the nation's second largest employer with 6.3 million workers ensures that its future as a major U.S. employer will be equally impressive.

The appeal of the travel and tourism industry as an employer is due not only to the quantity of jobs it provides, but to the diversity and quality of the jobs, as well. The $417 billion travel industry provides a myriad of opportunities within such segments as airlines, rental car companies, attractions and amusement parks, travel agencies, hotel companies, national parks, tour operators, cruise lines, restaurants, railways, and campgrounds. Even within these segments, a variety of jobs exist whether one chooses to start as a front-line worker, in management, or on the corporate side of the organization.

The industry's rapidly rising need for talented employees has contributed to the overall quality of the jobs the industry has to offer. Travel and tourism related jobs defy traditional stereotypes about service industry jobs. They pay well and provide excellent opportunities for advancement, training, and even ownership; and they are rapidly growing in number. In fact employment directly generated by travel has grown 56.3 percent in the last ten years—

far outperforming total U.S. employment (nonagricultural)—and promises to grow more than 30 percent in major travel industry sectors over the next twelve years. This compares very favorably to other U.S. industries such as construction, which is projected to grow 18 percent, and manufacturing, which is forecast to decline by 3 percent. Total U.S. employment grew only 21 percent over the same period of time and is projected to grow approximately the same amount over the next twelve years.

Today's travel industry has something for everyone. Consumers' interest in, enjoyment of, and need for our product continues to grow, which bodes well for the industry's future. Also, rapid changes in technology and communications are fueling major changes in how the travel industry does business. These advances are tearing down barriers and opening doors to the world marketplace, creating even more growth opportunities. In turn these growth opportunities are generating a greater need for a talented, educated, and multilingual workforce to move this exciting industry forward.

William S. Norman
President & CEO
Travel Industry Association of America

THOUGHTS ON TRAVEL
AND TOURISM

The worldwide importance of the travel and tourist industry is recognized and indicated by the statements of leaders at national and international levels.

Dr. Samuel I. Porrath, founder of The Institute of Transportation, Travel, and Tourism, Niagara University, New York:

> TTT (travel, transportation, and tourism) is an interfusion of industries that creates one of the world's most fascinating businesses. TTT is an amalgam of intercontinental enterprises, all of them growing rapidly and expanding daily, thus promising a strong, energetic future to those embracing it. TTT industries look for dedicated, management-level, university trained, academically prepared professionals equipped with the proper backgrounds for their multifaceted universal interests.

Kurt Waldheim, former Secretary General of the United Nations:

> Mutual understanding among the peoples of the world is a vital prerequisite for the evolution of friendly relations among states and the promotion of international cooperation. Tourism has become one of the most important factors in establishing and developing international cooperation and goodwill. Each year countless numbers of people take their

holidays abroad and meet people from other nations. In this way, they have a chance to learn about everyday life in other parts of the world and to come to a better understanding of different cultures. This can help them to respect other people's customs and attitudes. At the same time, people in the host country develop interest in their visitors' home countries; as with all human and international relations, tourism is not a one-way street but equally involves both sides. The United Nations recognized this highly important role of tourism long ago and together with its Specialized Agencies, has been promoting tourism through national and regional programs for years.

Tourists, in their travels, find not only rest and relaxation, but can make an important contribution to international understanding among the peoples of the world.

Ronald Reagan, former President of the United States:

The tourism industry is extremely important to the United States, contributing to our employment, economic prosperity, and international trade and understanding.

Each of us benefits from the effects of tourism. It substantially enhances our personal growth and education. Tourism also promotes intercultural understanding and appreciation of the geography, history, and people of the United States. Now that inflation has been reduced and the economy is growing, personal incomes and leisure time will increase more rapidly. Tourism therefore can be expected to play an even greater role in the lives of the American people.

DEDICATION

And now I see with eye serene,
The very pulse of the machine;
A being breathing thoughtful breath,
A traveler betwixt life and death;
The reason firm, the temperate will,
Endurance, foresight, strength, and skill;
A perfect woman, nobly planned,
To warn, to comfort, and command;
And yet a spirit still, and bright
With something of angelic light.

William Wordsworth

For Gaby, the pulse of my machine.

CHAPTER 1

OVERVIEW OF THE TRAVEL AND TOURISM INDUSTRY

As of 1996, travel has long been one of the three largest retail businesses in the United States. If *travel* is defined as trips at least one hundred miles from home and requiring an overnight stay, then travel was the third-largest retail business as of 1995; if shorter pleasure trips are included, it was the largest. There originally was some confusion in the common uses of the words *travel, transportation,* and *tourism.* This confusion was aggravated in the period of America's early affluence, when some tourists who had acquired riches before they acquired culture made themselves ridiculous by their uncouth manners, loud voices, and conspicuous consumption, particularly when they were traveling in Europe. As a result, many tourists preferred to be called *travelers,* and tourist agencies became *travel agencies,* tourist bureaus became *visitors' bureaus,* and so forth.

Today, this artificial distinction has largely eroded away, and these words can now be used with their real meanings. A tourist no longer feels insulted to be called a tourist, and numerous governmental offices call themselves tourist promotion bureaus.

Arbitrary but interesting definitions of these words are used at Niagara University (New York) in the Institute of Transportation, Travel, and Tourism (TTT). At TTT, *transportation* is defined as the movement of goods; *travel* is defined as the movement of people; and *tourism* concerns the entire business of leisure travel and related supporting activities.

This book concentrates on careers in all three of these broad fields, but selects those in which the work requires travel, direct service to travelers or vacationers, or promotion of travel and destinations. Thus, we shall discuss careers in the merchant marine because they entail travel, even though 97 percent of the workers on United States oceangoing ships are on tankers and freighters, and only 3 percent are on passenger ships. We shall omit consideration of workers in such fields as aircraft and automobile manufacture and auto repair. They serve the traveling public, but not directly, and little or no travel is required for their work.

ORIGIN AND DEVELOPMENT OF TRAVEL

Travel has always been an important feature of people's lives. Historically, what we would call business travel began, in the most primitive sense, with staying alive—travel to obtain food. As civilization advanced, travel became a means to promote trade, consolidate governments, and provide communication.

Great migrations of peoples took place after such disasters as lava flows or floods had devastated their lands. This was business travel of the purest sort—they had to find new lands that would support them. Nomads in semiarid lands seldom stayed long in one place because their grazing animals would soon consume all the vegetation. Many groups of people who herded animals, such as the Laplanders with their reindeer, moved twice every year between summer pastures and winter havens.

As people began to specialize in what they could grow or make or mine from the earth, trade developed. The first traveling salespeople were emissaries to find markets for goods and to arrange for caravans or ships to deliver these goods.

Military travel also developed early, as warlike tribes conquered peaceful ones and moved into their territories. As empires grew, soldiers traveled ceaselessly between the capital and the farthest borders to supervise and carry orders and to impose the ruler's will. Regular messenger systems became fast and reliable as early as ancient times in Egypt, developing over the millennia into stagecoach and packet boat networks, the Pony Express, and modern courier and postal systems.

Thus, the stream of travelers has grown constantly—sailors, ox-cart drivers, herdkeepers, messengers, salespeople, armies, covered-wagon trains—all intent on carrying on their own work or someone else's.

Another kind of travel developed in medieval times—educational travel. A young person learning a craft was apprenticed to a master craftsperson near home for a period of years to learn the basics; then the apprentice spent a year traveling to the workshops of masters of the craft in other countries, working there for a time to gain more skill and knowledge. Upon returning from these travels, the apprentice became a journeyman—one who had traveled and learned. Similarly, the typical university student spent a wander-year visiting universities in other countries, studying under the most illustrious professors to be found and polishing skills in one or two foreign languages. Travel thus achieved a new dimension, being performed not only for essential purposes, but to improve skill and knowledge.

Other nonbusiness travel was done for health reasons. Ancient Romans traveled to spas in Italy, Austria, and France seeking remedies for their ailments in curative water or mud. Only the wealthy could do this, of course, but physicians for hundreds of years have been prescribing travel as one way of improving health. They found that a change of air, of climate, of associations made people feel stronger. Europe's spas, which fell out of favor with American doctors as medical practice grew more scientific in the twentieth century, are not only still in business, but are attracting more people than ever before, including the patients of American doctors.

Travel for the pure pleasure of it—tourism—has been one of the special privileges of the rich since ancient times. Europe's spas, in addition to being health centers, were also social centers, with balls, picnics, plays, and concerts. They became more and more popular after stagecoaches were replaced by comfortable trains and sailing vessels by reliable steamships.

In America, too, there was summer travel by the rich to spas in Virginia, Pennsylvania, and Arkansas, as well as to summer estates at the seashore or in the mountains. The grand tour of Europe, which had become a tradition for aristocratic British students upon their graduation from Oxford or Cambridge, became a fashionable once-in-a-lifetime excursion of six months to a year for America's new industrial, mining, and railroad millionaires.

Wars have also stimulated travel. The Crusades, for example, gave Europe an interest in the Middle East that lasted for centuries, with trade and business travel flourishing between military campaigns. It was World War I that really brought intercontinental travel down to prices that middle-class Americans could afford, travel having piqued the interest of the millions of Americans who went to Europe to fight. Steamships were in their heyday, and the war had built up their passenger-carrying capacities.

At the same time, wide-ranging domestic travel came within the reach of Americans with the proliferation of inexpensive automobiles and hard-surfaced roads. As the automobile enabled people to travel further afield, such expensive resorts as Lakewood and Cape May, New Jersey, to which the wealthy had traveled by train from nearby cities, suddenly lost trade. Florida and southern California became destinations for mass travel, and many people began to travel during the winter to good mountain slopes for skiing. As a result, there began a burgeoning of beach, mountain, and ski resorts.

Then came World War II. Many millions of young American men and women were sent to Britain and all over Europe, to Hawaii, Alaska, the Philippines, China, India, Australia and New Zealand, the islands of the Pacific, North Africa and the Middle East, and finally, to conquered Japan, Germany, and Italy. These young people were fascinated with what they saw and did in other lands, and, naturally, they wanted to go back.

During the war years, aviation had come into its own. After the war, aerial troop transports were converted to serve the new traveling public as passenger aircraft, giving Americans a new kind of opportunity—travel to Europe for a vacation of only two weeks. United States aircraft factories converted to the manufacture of passenger planes and soon were supplying them to the new airlines that were springing up all over the world.

Travel now was possible for just about any American who wanted it—in their own cars throughout most of North America, or on low-priced excursion and charter flights to other continents. Worldwide tourism increased 1,000 percent from 1950 to 1970, a phenomenal advance. To support this increase, there had to be a commensurate increase in the infrastructure that sustains tourism and attracts tourists—hotels, gambling casinos, amusement parks, marinas, airports, highways, beach facilities, ski resorts, aircraft, buses, cars, restaurants, entertainment and sports facilities, rental cars and boats, and a host of less visible items such as electricity, gas, telephone, and water supply systems in resort areas.

War-torn Germany and Japan, starting from rock bottom in 1946, worked hard and built their economies into powerful positions within twenty years. Profits filtered down, and soon German and Japanese tourists were being seen all over the world, along with British, French, and Italian tourists.

TOURISM

Tourism requires some affluence, along with the feeling that travel is a desirable and rewarding activity. There are still about three billion people in the world who have neither the incentive nor the means to travel because their lives are totally occupied with the struggle for survival. And in many countries citizens may have the intellectual curiosity and perhaps even the means to travel, but it is forbidden, except on the business of the government or on government-sponsored projects. United States citizens tend to take travel for granted, but we should bear in mind that to the world's economically depressed and politically suppressed majority, it is an unattainable luxury.

Travel is coming to be regarded as a necessity in North America. Inflation in Europe and America, severe dollar devaluation, and an oil shortage imposed by the Arab nations reduced United States travel to Europe in 1974 by 10 to 15 percent from the level of just a few years before. But Americans did not stop traveling. During the severest part of the oil shortage, people went to resorts near home, and many of these recreational areas had record years. The oil shortage eased, but unemployment and inflation worsened during the winter of 1974–75, yet Florida and other southern areas were jammed with tourists.

Dr. Louis F. Twardzik, chairman of the Department of Park and Recreation Resources at Michigan State University, said:

> The great number of tourists crowding Florida resorts this winter wasn't really an unnatural phenomenon in times of social stress. Instead, it is merely an expression of the high value people place on their recreation today. The economic picture is severe enough to trigger a higher demand for recreation by people at all economic levels.

In the oil shortage of 1979, the earlier pattern was repeated. Travel in personal autos was considerably reduced, but this brought bonanza tourist business to resorts close to the cities. For longer journeys travelers again crowded into buses, ships, trains, and aircraft.

Two points are of importance to the person considering a career in travel. First, recreational travel, available only to the rich during most of the world's history, has come to be regarded as a necessity in the United States and Canada for people of the lower middle class as well as for those of the middle and upper classes. It is very broadly based. Second, if travel by certain modes or to certain destinations becomes too expensive or otherwise difficult, people will switch to other modes or destinations, but they will continue to travel for pleasure. This indicates stability for the industry as a whole, regardless of ups and downs for particular segments.

From 1985 on, it was noticed that people were taking more vacations, albeit shorter ones. Analysts deduced that this resulted from several changes in American life. In many families both husband and wife were working, which made it somewhat more difficult to get away for the traditional two weeks. There were more childless families, which made it easier to take spontaneous long-weekend vacations. There was less total leisure time because many people were working at two jobs, so they had to squeeze in brief vacations as their jobs permitted. The total effect on the tourism business was good, because it helped to even out the number of people on vacation at any one time, thus contributing more stability to the business and steadier work for its employees. From 1985 to 1987, weekend trips increased by 46%.

GROWTH AND STABILITY IN THIS FIELD

In 1995 the Travel Industry Association of American (TIA) reported the value of the United States travel industry at $417 billion, a very rapid increase from the $61 billion reported in 1975 and the $115 billion noted in 1979. From 1985 to 1989, foreign tourism in the United States jumped 49 percent, according to the TIA. One very happy result was that foreign visitors spent almost half a billion dollars more in the United States in 1989 than Americans spent abroad. This was the first travel-trade surplus for the United States. Tourism is thus the nation's largest export industry. It's also the nation's second largest employer, with 6.3 million employees.

Of the 6.3 million Americans directly employed in travel, TIA says that 52.9 percent are women, 11.2 percent are Black, and 8.8 percent are Hispanic.

The American Society of Travel Agents (ASTA) recently announced results of a survey showing that, for the average American family, travel-related expenditures rank second only to expenditures for groceries. ASTA also found that tourism is the first-, second-, or third-ranking industry in forty-six states in the Continental United States. In Hawaii, tourism generates more income than the main export products, sugar and pineapple. In the U.S. Virgin Islands, three-quarters of the area's total income is from tourism. Florida, California, and such other "sun spots" as the Mississippi Gulf Coast and the Texas coast depend heavily upon tourism. You may be surprised to learn that heavily industrialized New Jersey finds that tourism is its second most important industry. On every sunny summer day, New Jersey has more than a million people on its 128 miles of beautiful beaches.

Travel is one of the major industries of the United States, and in many countries of the world, it is by far the major industry. In coming decades, steadily increasing leisure time, greater longevity and earlier retirement age will make it more and more important. Beyond the fact that travel is a huge and strong industry that should afford a good degree of stability in travel-related work, it has a great intangible attraction. People in travel jobs are helping other people to go somewhere special, where they will relax and enjoy themselves. In our sedentary society, there are many who travel to find a challenge for their bodies—skiing, surfing, scuba diving, or mountain climbing.

With equal zest, others travel to find the challenges to the mind that appear in contrasting one's own feelings and actions with those of people in another country. Most groups believe they are inherently superior to others. Travelers refresh themselves in the discovery that theirs is not the only way of life, that they can learn from other cultures, that their habits and thoughts are not even acceptable to many people. They also find that they can contribute an occasional workable idea in a foreign setting.

The travel worker, whose hours are passed with travelers seeking physical and mental challenge, relaxation, and change, finds constant stimulation from working with travelers and helping them fulfill their desires. Helping others travel stimulates one's own urge to go places, and being in the industry gives one special advantages for personal travel.

PERKS IN THE TRAVEL INDUSTRY

A special inducement offered by careers in travel is the possibility of traveling oneself—at nominal cost, or totally free, or, better still, being paid to travel. Constant travel with a salary can be enjoyed as a member of a flight crew or a ship's company. Paid seasonal travel is available to tour directors—usually men and women who have worked their way up in a travel agency. Long-haul bus drivers, hostesses, and railroad train crews also are paid for constant travel.

Employees of airlines, passenger shipping lines, passenger rail lines, and bus lines, whether they travel in their jobs or not, usually are given liberal free or reduced-rate personal travel for themselves and their immediate families, beginning soon after they start working.

Travel agency personnel are so important in bringing business to air, rail, ship, and bus companies that these carriers offer them trips at very low rates and may offer free trips to familiarize them with new routes or cruises. Operators of tourist resorts or attractions and national tourism offices of foreign countries also give free familiarization trips to travel agents and sometimes to their staffs. Very low hotel rates usually are available to travel agency personnel. Additionally, employees of hotel chains, when traveling, usually can stay at their company's hotels at a fraction of the regular rates.

OPPORTUNITIES FOR WOMEN

Travel is one of the best career fields for women. Air travel, for example, developed the position of stewardess (now generally called flight attendant) giving women an opportunity for a glamorous position, a chance to meet all sorts of people under good conditions, and practically unlimited travel.

Many ticket agents for airlines, trains, buses, and all kinds of attractions are women. Women work in travel agencies, in public relations offices, and in many departments of hotels. Women are rangers and interpreters in national parks, lifeguards and recreation directors at pools and beaches and parks, and they do most of the office work that must take place in connection with every enterprise in the field of travel.

More than this, however, women are moving up in the travel industry. They are becoming officers of corporations that own hotels; department managers in all sorts of resort, amusement, and hotel enterprises; and many have gone out on their own to perform services independently. Among the latter are freelance travel writers, operators of travel agencies, owners of travel attractions, and operators of guide services. Many women now successfully run their own public relations firms. A few women have become airline captains, and many more are on their way to that rarefied position.

THE BROAD VARIETY OF TRAVEL JOBS

Transportation, travel, and tourism provide work for about one person in eight in the United States and Canada. The variety of occupations within the field or closely allied to it is almost without limit. For example, a doctor, a manicurist, a chef, and a horn player all become part of the travel business if they work on a ship, or at a resort such as Walt Disney World.

The travel world, therefore, is not a single profession or vocation, but dozens of professions and occupations. Education for travel-related work is thus of many different kinds, and there is no single way to prepare oneself for all travel jobs.

As in all large business organizations, marketing is vital to all of the major airlines, cruise lines, bus lines, hotel chains, and travel agencies. At the New School for Social Research in New York, the first master's degree program in Tourism and Travel Administration stresses marketing. The students, midcareer people working in travel, flock to the marketing courses. Marketing includes selling, but goes beyond salesmanship to find out what consumers want, why they prefer one product or hotel or airline over another, and much more. The effects on sales of public relations, advertising, merchandising, pricing, economics, airline scheduling, government regulation, and many other factors must be considered by a marketing director. A bachelor's degree with a major in marketing earns a job as marketing research trainee at about $24,000 per year. A senior marketing analyst averages around $41,000, and a director of marketing research may earn $79,000 or more. Talented marketing people are directly in line to become vice-presidents and presidents of their firms.

In the pages that follow, travel industries will be considered, one at a time, and the main career opportunities in each industry will be analyzed, their educational preparation will be discussed, and specific steps for getting started will be detailed.

CHAPTER 2

AIRLINES

The scheduled airlines of the United States form a gargantuan industry, transporting more than 470 million passengers and more than 13 billion ton-miles of freight and mail every year. This is accomplished with the investment of more than $75 billion in aircraft and ground facilities and the dedicated service of more than 540,000 employees.

Pay is fairly high in airline jobs, and working conditions are usually good. Since continued growth of the industry is expected, future prospects for employment are bright. It must be noted, however, that when faced with operating losses caused by skyrocketing fuel costs, economic recession, or other factors, many airlines cut out unprofitable routes or reduce service and, therefore, suspend hiring. Should the energy situation worsen, there could be reductions in service, with a consequent reduced need for new personnel. This would be temporary, however, since expanding population alone is bound to necessitate increasing air traffic. Airline work is exciting, and the industry is still growing. The field tends to attract adventurous people, so you are likely to discover social rewards in working with other lively and interesting employees.

FLIGHT ATTENDANTS

This position used to be referred to as *stewardess, hostess,* or *steward.* In the past, the employees who served food and drink and attended to passengers' wants on United States and Canadian airlines had to be female, unmarried, young, attractive, and (in the early days of aviation) short—because of the low ceilings in passenger craft. At first, airline companies also required that stewardesses be nurses.

There had been male stewards on some European airlines for many years, but most United States and Canadian lines preferred young women because they glamorized air travel and attracted passengers. However, a young man who was refused a stewardess job by an airline sued the company, charging sexual discrimination. He was upheld by the court, and since then, the airlines have had to consider both men and women eligible for positions as flight attendants. By 1979, about 25 percent of American flight attendants were male.

Other job qualifications have also changed. A woman no longer must be unmarried to be a flight attendant, but she does have to be willing to live in a city designated by the airline by which she is employed. The flight attendant need not be short, because aircraft ceilings are much higher than in years past. Pillows, blankets, and small luggage are stowed in overhead cabinets or racks, and attendants must be tall enough to reach them. There are some variations in most of these qualifications, so if you don't fit a certain airline's specifications, look for an airline that fits yours. Trans World Airlines says flight attendants of either sex can be 5'2" to 6'2" tall. United Airlines wants flight attendants 5'2" to 6'0" in height, as does Delta Air Lines. Air Canada's limits are 5'2" and 6'1". The acceptable weight of the applicant is expressed as "in proportion to height" by most airlines, although some of them define this with a listing of the maximum weight acceptable at specific heights. Minimum age for flight attendants varies from 19 to 20 (Delta, United, TWA, for example) to 21. Air Canada has no age limitation, but requires a year of work experience.

Most airlines require flight attendants to be high school graduates, although some say something such as, "A high school diploma or G.E.D., while not required, is preferred." In actuality, most airlines want people who have had two years of college, nursing training, or experience in dealing with the public.

"United States immigration policy in most cases prevents us from considering anyone who is not a United States citizen or an alien with a permanent visa." This is true of all United States airlines. Since most airlines have a policy of hiring their own nationals, it is difficult for an American or Canadian to get a job with a European airline, for example, unless he or she has some special required qualification such as fluency in several languages. Excellent English is expected by all airlines, and if you hope to work on an international route, you should have "a fair background in one other language." Air Canada requires its flight attendants to be Canadian citizens or landed immigrants. Those serving in Quebec must be fluent in both English and French and ability in other languages is desirable.

Vision should be good, and if it needs correction, the airlines prefer contact lenses. United, TWA, and Air Canada accept flight attendants who wear glasses, but Delta does not. Several airlines mention that if contacts are worn, they should have been used successfully by the candidate for at least half a year before applying for the job. The airlines have varying requirements as to minimum visual acuity.

General health should be excellent, including hearing. Most airlines give flight crews regular flight physical examinations to make sure they remain in good condition and ready to cope with emergencies.

All the airlines stress the importance of good appearance. Delta says:

> The main qualities Delta interviewers look for in flight attendant applicants are a neat, wholesome appearance and the ability to project themselves and their personality. Airline flight attendants have a public relations as well as a service job. Their responsibility is to care for passengers on their flight in such a way that passengers will prefer Delta Air Lines over any other mode of transportation.

TWA wants its flight attendants to have:

> ... an attractive appearance, poise and a natural ability to communicate, and flexibility as it relates to job assignment...a mature and self-starting individual who has the ability to work well under pressure and still maintain concern for people.

Air Canada declares:

> We look for people who are attractive, natural, and spontaneous, with an ability to anticipate the needs of our customers. The airline business is a very competitive one and satisfying our customers' needs is a way of showing that we really care.

Training

Various private schools offer specialized training for flight attendant jobs, but generally speaking, such programs are not likely to help get you a job. Every airline either operates its own training facilities or sends its new flight attendants to a school, sometimes operated by another airline with which it has a contract. Training by the airlines is of four to six weeks' duration.

TWA trains its student flight attendants at Breech Training Academy in Overland Park, Kansas. TWA's school has 300 guest rooms, with two students sharing each room.

United says the following about their program:

> Those selected complete a 4½-week training program at our modern Training Center located in suburban Chicago. During this period, trainees are instructed in a variety of subjects that include aircraft familiarization, communications, food services, emergency procedures, passenger relations, and personal appearance. The selection process continues during training and the subsequent six-month probationary period.

TWA charges $2,995 for training, which can be financed. It describes its training program as follows:

> During the five-week training course, your instructors are all line flight attendants capable of relating to your individual questions. In training you will become knowledgeable in the areas of safety and aircraft. You will learn about our fleet of aircraft. Aircraft mock-ups will be available to you for training purposes. In addition, you will be going on observation flights, as well as actually working on flights in order to prepare yourself for your new position. Along with the aircraft training, you will learn emergency safety procedures which will serve to develop your self-confidence in handling any emergency situation.
>
> After becoming proficient in aircraft and safety, you will begin classes in the service area. Instruction in this area entails everything from serving a cocktail to preparing a chateaubriand with poise and confidence.
>
> Throughout the training period, you will be involved in classes pertaining to corporate awareness, personal development, customer service concepts, and appearance and grooming techniques.

Delta conducts its flight attendant training school at Hartsfield Atlanta International Airport, Atlanta, Georgia. Students are instructed and housed in the same building. During training, school is in session from 8 to 5, with plenty of study to do every evening and a midnight curfew. The three weekends are taken up with observation flights.

Delta says:

> A substantial portion of the training program is devoted to physical fitness and good grooming, and the Training Center reflects this emphasis. A complete beauty parlor is part of the large make-up room where trainees learn to style their hair and to accentuate [their] best features through proper use of cosmetics. Exercise equipment is available for those who want to use it.
>
> The first week of study is devoted to physical examinations, uniform fittings, grooming instruction, general introductory briefings on Delta history and policy, and enough fundamental aircraft nomenclature to get the trainees through the following weeks of specialized study of each individual Delta plane.
>
> During the course they also learn basic flight theory... and the jurisdiction and function of governmental agencies and all other agencies even remotely touching on airline operation.
>
> Among facilities for safety procedures is a specially equipped balcony from which trainees receive realistic training by actually operating and sliding down an emergency evacuation chute.
>
> To practice in-flight service, trainees use still another area, an aircraft mock-up, which contains 29 seats (21 tourist and 8 first class), fully equipped galley, public address system, panels for lighting and air conditioning, and coat closet. They practice meal service by serving each other. A successful service is quite an exciting event. It's also fun, for the trainees get to eat the meals, representative of what they will soon be

serving on their own flights. They practice voice improvement and correct diction, ready for the day when they will be making flight announcements over their plane's public address system.

Instructors are Delta stewardesses who have been flying for several years. They are attractive, knowledgeable, and experienced. The curriculum is complex, but there is a very low failure rate. Graduation is a reward of the 4-week course, and smart new uniforms are trimmed with Delta wings.

American Airlines gives flight attendants five weeks of training near Fort Worth, Texas. Instruction includes medical procedures, such as resuscitation, and how to deal with hijackers.

The Air Canada Training Center, in Montreal, has a four-week program teaching technical aspects of the line's aircraft, safety and emergency procedures, and the importance of a customer. There is realistic training in aircraft mock-ups.

Work Locations

The home base at which a flight attendant lives most of the time is called the domicile. This is not a dormitory, but a city in which the employee has an apartment. TWA's international flight attendants are domiciled in New York, Paris, and Los Angeles, and its domestic flight attendants are based in those cities and in Boston and St. Louis. United's domiciles are in New York, Newark, Washington, Miami, Honolulu, Chicago, Denver, Los Angeles, San Francisco, and Seattle. Delta bases are in Atlanta, Boston, Chicago, Dallas, Los Angeles, Cincinnati, Salt Lake City, and New Orleans. Air Canada's in-flight services bases are at Vancouver, Calgary, Winnipeg, Toronto, Montreal, and Halifax.

At United, "New flight attendants are assigned to fill domicile openings by preference bidding based upon chronological age."

After nine months at the first domicile, they may request transfer, but seniority rules, so "it may be several years before being able to relocate to our domiciles on the West Coast or Hawaii." At TWA, however, "Newly graduated flight attendants are assigned to available domicile openings according to company requirements and must be willing to relocate to one of these domiciles after training. After the 6-month probationary period, you may bid to other domiciles based on flight attendant seniority."

If you want to remain permanently in the same city, try an airline with short routes—generally called *feeder* lines—where there's a good chance of your getting home to the same bed every night. On the long routes, you are likely to spend several nights each month in a hotel room at the far end of the route.

At Delta:

> For the first few weeks after graduation, new flight attendants are on "reserve." This means that instead of having regular flights, they are on standby basis and must be available on designated reserve days to fill in whenever and wherever they are needed. They are soon given the opportunity to "bid" each month on the routes they would like to fly. Since seniority is the deciding factor, new flight attendants usually have to wait for what they consider choice assignments. The probationary period is six months.

Air Canada says:

> While new flight attendants are assigned to a base where vacancies exist, they may request a change of location at any time thereafter. Transfers are obtained on the basis of vacancies and flight attendant seniority, but may not be available for periods of two to three years; therefore applicants should be prepared to accept assignment to any base as permanent.

Employment and Salaries

The U.S. Department of Labor reports that there were 93,000 flight attendants employed in 1992. It projected keen competition for flight attendant positions through the year 2005, with the number of applicants exceeding the number of job openings, but job openings increasing by 59,000 because of increases in the number and size of planes. Applicants with some college training and experience dealing with the public will continue to have the best job prospects.

The U.S. Federal Aviation Administration views flight attendants not only as people who minister to passengers' creature comforts, but as guardians of passengers' safety. The FAA requires that there be one flight attendant for every fifty seats on an airliner, for passenger protection in case of emergencies. As aircraft grow in size, the number of flight attendants increases.

The Association of Flight Attendants, AFL-CIO, represents the airline attendants of a number of airlines. Attendants of other lines are represented by the Transport Workers' Union, AFL-CIO, and the International Brotherhood of Teamsters, Chauffeurs, Warehousemen & Helpers of America. Most flight attendants are union members.

In the late 1970s, the unions argued, bargained, and held long strikes. They succeeded in gaining recognition of their professionalism, higher pay, more consideration for their health and maternity problems, and improved rest facilities.

After the Airline Deregulation Act took effect at the beginning of 1985, however, the airline business was suddenly much more competitive than before. With no regulation of rates or routes or schedules, airlines were free to engage in rate wars, start new routes, drop service on routes losing money, and cut costs to the bone. One way of cutting costs was to reduce salaries. Continental did this, after much labor strife, by reducing salaries for new hires. Under the "A" scale, stewardesses started with base salary of $1,142 a month and could advance to a plateau of $2,306 over a twelve-year period. Newly hired people were paid under the "B" scale, starting at base pay of $972 and rising within five years to a plateau of $1,200.

Delta Airlines in 1990 was paying starting salaries of $12,000 to $15,000 a year. With many years of seniority and many over-time hours this could rise to $40,000–$50,000, especially for those who had become supervisors. According to a survey by the Association of Flight Attendants in 1992, covering thirty airlines, median starting pay was $13,000 a year. The median rate after six years on the job was around $20,000, and some senior flight atten-dants earned as much as $40,000 a year.

As part of the cost-cutting drive, some airlines started charging a fee for accepting a job application, charging new flight atten-dants for their uniforms, and charging tuition to attend the "charm farm" (flight attendant training school). The airlines also started scheduling flights closer together, so that a flight crew would have only a ten-hour layover between flights, instead of a twenty-four-hour respite. Competition among airlines mandated these changes, which led to higher productivity.

On international flights (where facility in a foreign language is always desired, and often required), pay ranges from 12 to 20 per-cent higher.

With most of the major airlines, there is base pay for the first sixty-five flying hours, and for each further flight hour, up to a maximum of eighty-five hours, there is additional pay. Pay raises are small but regular enough to be counted on, and there are al-lowances for meals away from home, limousines to and from air-ports, and uniform maintenance.

Advancement

Advancement from the position of flight attendant comes with seniority and merit. Top position in the cabin crew is flight service director. At some airlines there is a special position called purser, the person who handles all cash collected in flight for drinks, earphones, and merchandise.

Nonflying positions to which flight attendants can be promoted include jobs as instructor, customer service director, and recruiting representative. Flight attendants may model for photographs by the airline's public relations staff.

At Delta, which has historically insisted upon promotion from within, an example of promotion possibilities is provided by Norma Wildes. She joined Delta as a stewardess. After three years of flying out of Miami and Atlanta, she became secretary to Delta's director of engineering. Soon she was promoted to be one of five Delta female sales representatives, and within half a year became coordinator of women's services for the airline, overseeing the production of such travel information and services to women as a guide to efficient packing, recipe booklets, films showing secretaries and secretarial students how to book air reservations, and other projects to make travel by Delta appealing and easy for women.

Job Duties

In addition to serving meals and drinks, flight attendants have other duties. They board the flight early to check cabin equipment, adjust lighting and ventilation, and check supplies and meals before the passengers board. They hang up passengers' coats, see that carry-on luggage is properly stowed, check seatbelts, prevent smoking, and make flight announcements.

They also demonstrate emergency oxygen and flotation equipment and point out escape doors. Sarah Uzzel-Rindlaub, instructor in emergency procedures for United, has unique qualifications—she has survived two crashes and points out that survival depends on knowing procedures and acting fast.

Flight attendants also check passenger lists before takeoff, direct passengers to the proper seats, and take care of flight reports, caterers' invoices, and requests for supplies or for special attention to equipment.

Flight attendants must soothe angry, frightened, or sick passengers; serve drinks and meals as rapidly as possible; and take care of any special needs of passengers or the flight-deck crew. They often must work under tension, and on long trips, they may finish serving dinner at midnight and start serving breakfast two hours later. Vacation travel often starts Friday evening or Saturday morning and ends Sunday evening, so flight attendants often find themselves working in the sky instead of enjoying a Saturday-night date.

From the viewpoint of the Federal Aviation Administration, the flight attendants are on board for the safety of the passengers: to inform passengers of safety procedures and regulations and to enforce them. When a passenger becomes drunk and disorderly, or sick, or even goes crazy or dies, it is the flight attendants who must cope with the problems. When there's an emergency landing, flight attendants must deploy slides and evacuate passengers swiftly. And the flight attendant is usually the first person to deal with a hijacker.

On the other hand, flight attendants have considerable variety in their work and the added bonus of free or very inexpensive travel. In addition, they generally receive all the fringe benefits available in comparable office jobs.

PILOTS AND COPILOTS

A job whose glamour is equal to that of the flight attendant is airline *pilot.* In addition to their prestige, pilots are highly paid, up to $165,000 or more per year. This figure is rising as aircraft grow larger and more complicated.

There were 85,000 civilian pilots in 1992, and the Bureau of Labor Statistics forecasts another 31,000 by 2005. Job prospects for major airlines are best for college graduates who have a commercial pilot's license or flight engineer's license and experience flying jets.

Job Duties

The commercial airline pilot arrives at the airport well before takeoff time. After getting information from the meteorological office about weather conditions along the flight path, the pilot works out route, speed, and altitude in a conference with the airline dispatcher. He or she then coordinates this flight plan with the air traffic controllers. The copilot is generally with the pilot during these conferences and assists as requested in working out practical routes and altitudes.

They proceed to the airplane, where they check the controls, engines, and instruments, going down a long checklist item by item. Passengers board and are strapped in, the cabin-crew chief advises the pilot that they are ready, and the pilot obtains permission from air traffic control to taxi and then to take off. Once airborne and on course, the pilot or copilot makes frequent radio reports to controllers on the ground as to the plane's altitude, speed, and position; the weather; amount of fuel remaining; and anything unusual about the flight. Altitude and speed are changed, as well as the plane's heading, as the pilot deems necessary. Instruments detailing condition of engines, amount of fuel, altitude, airspeed, and other factors are constantly scrutinized.

In case of an emergency, such as an engine's becoming too hot or ice forming on the wings faster than it can be melted, the captain must take time, distance, fuel, and other factors into consideration. Shutting down one engine, for example, will make it take longer to reach the destination. If low fog or clouds obscure the field at the destination, an approach on instruments may be necessary, with a controller on the ground "talking the plane down." Leaving the aircraft after the flight, the pilot and copilot must fill out records of the flight at the airline office before they have completed their day's work.

Some senior pilots become instructors. There is a considerable need for them because every time an airline starts using a new model of airplane, pilots must be given instructions on how to fly it. Sometimes the first airline to start using a new model will instruct the pilots of several other airlines.

The FAA requires that each pilot's performance be evaluated at least twice each year. Senior pilots take specialized training to become evaluators so they can check out other pilots.

Not all pilots in the travel trade fly large passenger planes. Some of them are *bush pilots* who still "fly by the seat of their pants" to wilderness lakes, perhaps carrying a couple of fishermen whose canoe is lashed to the undercarriage of the floatplane. Skiers are borne to the tops of otherwise inaccessible mountains by helicopter or ski plane pilots, so they can ski down over miles of virgin snow. Single-engine aircraft tow gliders up 3,000 or 4,000 feet above ground level and release them to soar in the empyrean. Sport parachutists are taken aloft; then they jump out and aim for ground targets. Many pilots are employed by corporations to fly executives on business trips.

There are also many very small airlines, operating a few one- or two-engine planes to island resorts, offshore gambling havens, camps in the woods, and other places where there is a continuous but small stream of travelers. As an example, Scenic Airlines in Las Vegas flies tourists on a sight-seeing trip up the Grand Canyon, lands them on the rim for a ground tour, and flies them back to Las Vegas in the sunset. In such an operation, the pilot may conduct the ground tour, pick up the passengers from their hotels, and also perform the aircraft maintenance. He or she has considerable independence when airborne, but much less support from the ground than has the pilot of a commercial airline.

More and more women are becoming pilots, gaining experience and flying hours as flying instructors and air taxi pilots. A few of them have worked their way into the airlines. The fact that the airlines prefer pilots with military training has made it difficult for women to break in, but as the military services admit more women to their flight programs, more women will also become airline pilots.

Requirements

Safe flying is the major ability demanded by airlines of their pilots. Punctuality for on-time departures and arrivals also is desirable, but safety is always paramount. Heroes are really not desired in this job. Airlines prefer steady, eminently well-qualified people who take pride in their own perfectionism as they check out equipment, weather, and all the many items that might possibly go wrong and cause trouble in flight. In addition to being a perfectionist, a pilot must be cool in emergencies. Previous flying experience, often in the military, will probably have subjected the pilot to many emergencies, perhaps in combat, where her or his mettle was tested and proved.

The actual minute-by-minute supervision of the aircraft in flight is not much work anymore. Whereas early pilots sometimes navigated by following highways and were lost when they got into fog, the modern pilot has all the advantages of radar and loran, radio compass, and many other helpful instruments. In addition, airline flight is monitored from the ground by flight controllers who can advise of the plane's precise position and warn about weather difficulties ahead, other aircraft in the path, or dangerously low altitude.

The pilot of past years controlled the plane's course constantly with a joystick; however, modern transport aircraft are flown mechanically during most of the flight, except during takeoff and landing. On most long flights, a minor compass correction once or twice an hour is about all that is needed to keep the aircraft in straight and level flight and on the shortest safe course to its destination. A computer makes all the tiny corrections that used to be made by a pilot's sensitive fingers on the joystick. But the pilot, copilot, and usually the flight engineer must be able to take control and fly the aircraft in any sort of emergency that might develop— from minor turbulence, to losing an engine, to diving the plane down to safe altitude if the cabin is ruptured and depressurized.

Most of the pilot's skill and ability are almost never used, but are held in reserve in case of need. For people who want continual challenge to which they can respond vigorously, this kind of work can be frustrating. An airline pilot does not have the exciting fight against fate and elements that Charles Lindbergh had. Instead, he or she spends long hours just keeping an eye on things.

At the beginning and end of every flight, however, the pilot earns that high pay, by lifting the monstrous machine into the air and bringing it safely back to earth. The pilot often is called the *captain* by the airlines. Like the captain of a ship, he or she has total responsibility for the safety of passengers, crew, and cargo. In the air, all passengers, as well as the flight crew, are subject to her or his orders. The copilot often is called *first officer* by the airlines, and the flight engineer *second officer.* In most airlines the captain wears four sleeve stripes, the first officer three, and the flight engineer two.

Many licenses are required for pilots and copilots. The FAA administers a flight physical for the commercial pilot's license to people with a minimum of 250 hours of flight time. Then a written test is given on FAA regulations, navigation in the air, flight safety, and other subjects. Finally, pilots are given a flying test, with an examiner aboard the plane.

This license is qualified so that the pilot is permitted to fly only single-engine, multiengine, or floatplanes. It is further qualified for the particular types of aircraft on which the pilot has been checked out.

An airline transport pilot's license is required for airline captains. To get this, a person must have an instrument rating, which requires flying under instrument conditions for forty hours or more. One must be at least twenty-three years of age, with 1,500 hours or more of flight time in the previous eight years.

The commercial license is valid as long as the flier can pass the annual physical and semiannual flight evaluation, but no pilot over sixty years old is permitted to fly an airliner. At or before this age, many pilots are transferred to ground duties, usually in operations. Pilots have been contesting this rule.

The airlines publish minimum requirements, but all of them add something such as this advice:

> Competition has been quite intense. The majority of candidates seeking employment possess a bachelor's degree, plus have jet or turbo-prop training and experience. Typically, they have well in excess of 1,500 total flight hours.

Delta strongly suggests getting a bachelor's degree, then joining the Air Force, Navy, Marines, or Army for flight training: "A great majority of Delta's pilots receive their flight training in military service."

This is true throughout the airline industry. Learning to fly in a civilian flying school is possible, but costly, and it could be difficult acquiring the 1,500 hours of flight time required for the transport license. In time of war, when the military is using all the pilots it can get, the airline industry would no doubt take new pilots with minimum qualifications or even less than minimum. But during times of peace, when there are thousands of pilots looking for flying jobs, the airlines can take their pick, and they naturally choose the most highly qualified.

United's basic qualifications are as follows: age, 21–35; 350 hours experience in fixed-wing aircraft; high school diploma; FAA commercial pilot certificate with instrument rating; vision, 20/70 correctable to 20/20; height sufficient to operate all controls; second class FAA medical certificate and ability to obtain first class certificate; United States citizen or permanently domiciled alien status. Those selected must pass the FAA flight engineer written exams (basic and turbojet) before commencing training by United.

At Delta, the minimum requirements are as follows: age, 21; height, 5'8"; weight in proportion to height; college degree preferred; first-class physical; FAA instrument rating; FAA commercial license; FCC restricted radiotelephone license; fixed-wing multiengine flight experience preferred.

Air Canada's minimum requirements are as follows: age, 20 or above; schooling at least to university entrance level and preferably higher; height, at least 5'6"; vision, at least 20/50 (correctable to 20/20); at least 300 hours flight time including 150 hours as pilot-in-command, 20 hours cross-country, 10 hours at night (etc.); at least a Canadian Commercial Pilot License with current

Class I Instrument Rating and Multiengine Endorsement; Canadian Radio Telephone (restricted) License; a Canadian citizen or landed immigrant. In addition to flying ability and good health, Air Canada looks for intelligence, emotional stability, alertness, and leadership qualities.

Very few people are hired to start as pilot (or captain) for the major airlines. Historically, most began as flight engineers, with eventual promotion to first officer and finally to captain. Nowadays, however, as flight engineers are being replaced by new technology, one's first job on the flight deck is as copilot. (Air Canada and United call their flight engineers second officers.) Reaction time and ability to make rapid correct judgments under stress are tested, and cockpit crew members must maintain excellent physical condition to keep their jobs.

Training

As wars slip into history and time passes, the number of aviators with military training decreases. The FAA has certified some 600 civilian flying schools to compensate for this. Among these are some colleges and universities that offer degree credit for pilot training. Airlines still prefer militarily trained pilots, but now must accept those with civilian training. The United States military has lost so many trained pilots to civilian work that it is hoping to curb this high attrition rate through special pay and bonuses. This will make the airlines more dependent upon civilian-trained aviators, or on their own training for pilots and copilots.

Before being allowed to take up passengers, the newly hired flight engineer, copilot, or pilot is given extensive training by the airline. This includes classroom instruction in meteorology, FAA regulations, and company policies and rules. Three to ten weeks of flight instruction consisting of lectures, time in simulated aircraft, and actual flights may also be given. A trainee who does not have a rating for the type of airplane he or she will be flying must earn it.

New Delta pilots have eight weeks of ground training in Atlanta, followed by thirty to forty-five days of flight training.

Air Canada gives its new pilots three to four months of training, including seven weeks of ground school followed by procedures trainer, simulator, and actual flight training. Initial assignment can be as first or second officer. United trains its new second officers up to fourteen weeks at its huge flight training center in Denver.

Delta pilots are based at Atlanta, Chicago, Boston, Dallas, Houston, Miami, and New Orleans. Air Canada's bases for pilots are in Montreal, Toronto, Winnipeg, and Vancouver. United bases its flight officers at Cleveland, Chicago, Denver, Los Angeles, Miami, New York, San Francisco, Seattle, and Washington.

Salaries

In 1992, average salary for pilots was $80,000, and captains earned an average of $107,000. Copilots were making an average of $65,000.

Airline pilots and copilots earn more than those employed by corporations or government. Most United States airline pilots are members of a union, the Air Line Pilots Association, International. The union representing Air Canada's pilots is the Canadian Air Line Pilots Association. Pilot pay is decided upon by bargaining between union and company.

Work schedules are irregular, since they are based on when the majority of people want to fly. Vacationers typically want to fly on weekends and during nonbusiness hours. Airline pilots, on average, are away from home bases overnight about one-third of the time. Airlines provide them hotel rooms and expense allowances for this.

The Federal Aviation Act forbids airline pilots and copilots to fly more than 100 hours per month or 1,000 hours per year. Most of them fly about 75 hours a month, but total hours on duty, including layover time before return flights, usually rise to 120.

Most pilots and copilots enjoy liberal vacations and other fringe benefits, including a considerable amount of free or low-cost personal travel. Joining an airline's cockpit crew is difficult, and keeping the job is challenging, but the responsibility, pay, and prestige make it well worthwhile.

The Department of Labor reported that 85,000 pilots were employed in 1992. Air travel is very sensitive to economic swings, however, and a recession always causes reduction in numbers of flights, and consequent crew layoffs. Restructuring of airlines in the nineties has reduced the need for pilots.

The average yearly need for new pilots is projected as several thousand. About half of all civilian pilots are commercial airline pilots, and the rest are pilots of corporation jets, aviation instructors, air taxi pilots, crop dusters, government inspectors, and others.

FLIGHT ENGINEERS

Whereas the *flight engineer* is at the bottom of the cockpit crew hierarchy, as noted in the section on pilots and copilots, he or she must be an expert on mechanics, engine overhaul, and aircraft electronics.

The flight engineer's job combines the fields of operations and maintenance of the aircraft. He or she is expected to be able to take over as captain of the plane if the pilot and copilot should in some way become unable to act. Promotion to copilot comes after two to seven years and to pilot after five to fifteen years, in accordance with seniority and union contract.

New large aircraft have flight-management computers that do much of the flight engineer's work, so when they can safely do so, the airlines get along without flight engineers.

Job Duties

The main practical operating responsibility of the flight engineer is to know every blade and bolt and valve, every spark plug, transistor, wire, pipe, and tank on the aircraft. The flight engineer's place in the cockpit is well supplied with instruments that report on every critical point and phase of engine operation, electronic systems, fuel and its flow, temperature, and many other conditions.

When any instrument or combination of instruments shows something unusual, the flight engineer must be able to diagnose trouble rapidly, report it immediately to the pilot, and, if possible, repair it in flight or arrange for removal of stress from an affected part until mechanics on the ground can repair it. If the next stop is at a small airport without mechanics trained for the particular type of aircraft, the flight engineer may well be the one to make the repair.

On a typical flight, the flight engineer joins the pilot and copilot in the preflight weather briefing and conference on route and altitude. Together they check the aircraft's maintenance record to be sure that needed overhauls and equipment replacement have been made as required. Arriving at the airplane, they inspect the exterior briefly, including the tires.

The flight engineer assists the pilot and copilot in making preflight checks of equipment, controls, and instruments in the cockpit. He or she checks fuel levels, electric power, and engine-report instruments. In flight, the flight engineer adjusts controls to keep the engines at maximum efficiency, records engine performance and fuel consumption at frequent intervals, and watches cabin pressure and temperature and adjusts them as necessary.

Personal Requirements and Training

The same physical and height and weight standards are required by the airlines for flight engineers as for pilots and copilots—and the same coolness under fire. A high school education is required, and some airlines require college as well.

The best way for flight engineers to obtain the necessary training is in the armed forces, just as for pilots and copilots. An FAA flight engineer's license is required. Qualification for this consists of three or more years' experience as a pilot or flight engineer in the armed forces, or in repair and overhaul of aircraft engines. A stiff flight physical examination and a written test on engine operation and the theory of flight are also required for this license, plus a flight check in an aircraft of the type to which the engineer seeks assignment. An applicant without armed services experience can study for the license at a private aviation school approved by the FAA. Also required is the commercial pilot's license described in the section on pilots and copilots.

Employment and Salaries

According to the U.S. Department of Labor, about 21,000 flight engineers were employed in the United States in 1990.

The earnings of flight engineers in 1994 averaged $42,000 a year, with bonuses sometimes given for night and international flights.

Not all flight engineers are pilots, but those who are belong to the Air Line Pilots Association, International. Most others belong to the Flight Engineers' International Association or International Brotherhood of Teamsters, Chauffeurs, Warehousemen and Helpers of America.

AIRCRAFT MECHANICS

One way in which a person can prepare to become a flight engineer is to first become an *aircraft mechanic.* There are almost twice as many aircraft mechanics as there are pilots, copilots, and flight engineers combined. Although the mechanics are seldom seen by the traveling public, there would be no flying without them.

There are three main specialties among aircraft mechanics: power plant, airframe, and repairer. In addition to doing such routine preventive maintenance as changing engine oil, greasing wheel bearings, and replacing spark plugs, aircraft mechanics dismantle engines, check all the parts for wear, and rebuild them. The FAA requires regular inspection of airframes and power plants. Repairers work on instruments and propellers. When a flight is delayed for emergency repairs, mechanics must work fast to get the plane back into the air.

Employment and Training

In 1992, 131,000 aircraft mechanics were employed in the United States. The Bureau of Labor Statistics expects there will be another 29,000 by 2005 because of increased air traffic. More than three-fifths of salaried mechanics were employed by the airlines. Approximately one-fifth worked for aircraft assembly firms, and nearly one-sixth were employed by the federal government. Many of the remaining mechanics worked in general aviation, usually for independent repair shops. More than half of all airline mechanics work at airports near New York, Houston, Oklahoma City,

Miami, Chicago, Los Angeles, San Francisco, and Dallas. An airline usually operates a major repair base for each type of aircraft in its system.

Training for most mechanics consists of graduation from high school or vocational school, plus some experience in a machine shop or auto repair shop. Major airlines operate apprenticeship programs of three or four years' duration, combining classroom and on-the-job training. Those who have been aircraft mechanics in the armed forces can complete their apprenticeship rapidly, or if they are fortunate enough to have worked with aircraft very similar to those the airline flies, they might step right into a mechanic's job. The FAA has a list of mechanic schools that it has approved, and they will make the list available to anyone who is interested. Programs at most of these schools are of one and a half to two years' duration.

Graduates of these schools, or mechanics with eighteen months of experience, are eligible to take the written and practical tests for a license as an airframe or power plant mechanic or as a repairer. A mechanic trying for both airframe and power plant licenses at once must have thirty months' experience. Airframe mechanics are qualified to work on wings, fuselages, and landing gear, while power plant mechanics work on engines. A mechanic who has had both licenses for at least three years may take examinations and be qualified as an *aircraft inspector,* after which he or she certifies the work of other mechanics.

Licensed mechanics advance with increasing seniority and ability to lead. A mechanic may become a crew chief, shop foreman, maintenance supervisor, and perhaps, company executive. Some start their own shops and work on contract for small airlines, corporations, government agencies, or other general aviation aircraft operators. Others learn to fly well enough to earn a commercial pilot's license and become flight engineers.

The airlines paid beginning aircraft mechanics $8.66 to $13.09 an hour in 1992. Experienced mechanics made between $15 and $25 an hour. Mechanics working for the federal government in 1993 earned an average of $35,200 a year.

In 1992, the median annual income for aircraft mechanics was approximately $32,500, with the top 10 percent of aircraft mechanics earning salaries of over $37,500 a year.

Additionally, free or low-cost travel on their own and other airlines, plus other fringe benefits, are standard.

Unions representing aircraft mechanics include the International Association of Machinists and Aerospace Workers, the Transport Workers Union of America, and the International Brotherhood of Teamsters, Chauffeurs, Warehousemen and Helpers of America.

TICKET AGENTS, RESERVATION AGENTS, AND CLERKS

Reservation agents and *clerks* for major airlines generally work in central offices. As the human link between the telephone and a computer terminal, the agent gives information on flight schedules and the availability of seats, and makes reservations. Agents receive calls from the general public, from travel agents, and from their company's ticket agents. They generally do not come face-to-face with customers, but do all their contact work by telephone.

Ticket agents work at ticket counters in airports and in central-city ticket offices. They answer questions about fares and schedules, give out timetables and descriptive literature, check directly with computers or with reservation agents for seat availability, and sell tickets, often by typing the passengers' names into the computer. Fares are so complicated in air travel that selling a ticket is a more difficult procedure than it might seem. Ticket agents check in and tag baggage, add any excess-baggage charges, and issue boarding passes to permit passengers to get to the airplanes. *Passenger agents* help airport ticket agents, help passengers board the aircraft, collect tickets, and in some cases assign seats. At United, these personnel are called *customer services clerk* (entry level) and *customer service agent.*

Ticket and passenger agents are as smartly uniformed as flight crews. They are selected on the basis of pleasing personality and appearance, good diction, and education. High school graduation generally is required, and two or more years of college preferred. Chances for advancement are improved by college courses in traffic management and other phases of transportation.

In 1992, according to the U.S. Department of Labor, the airlines employed about 131,000 reservation agents and ticket agents. Not much change is expected in these numbers, because improving computerization of ticketing and recordkeeping machines gradually accomplishes more and more of the work. However increases in airline travel will require another 52,000 ticket and reservations clerks by 2005, according to the Bureau of Labor Statistics.

The loading of baggage and cargo is supervised by *operations* or *station* or *ramp agents,* and sometimes even performed by them. They see that cargo weight is evenly distributed in the aircraft and keep cargo manifests and lists of numbers of passengers. They may also announce arrivals and departures.

Outside sales agents for the airlines often are called *traffic representatives.* They visit shippers and corporations, keeping present customers happy and trying to obtain new customers. Ticket and reservation agents may advance to supervisor in these specialties or to traffic representative.

Heading all sales efforts are *city sales managers,* and above them, *district sales managers.* The district sales manager administers ticket and reservations offices, directs the efforts of sales representatives, and promotes traffic on the airline.

More information on airline jobs may be obtained from the following sources:

Air Line Pilots Association, International
    1625 Massachusetts Avenue NW
    Washington, DC 20036-2283

Flight Engineers' International Association
    1926 Pacific Highway, #202
    Redondo Beach, CA 90277

Air Transport Association of America
    1301 Pennsylvania Avenue NW, #1100
    Washington, DC 20004

Future Aviation Professionals of America
    4959 Massachusetts Boulevard
    Atlanta, GA 30037

Air Line Employees Association
    Job Opportunity Program
    5600 South Central Avenue
    Chicago, IL 60638-3797

Air Canada
    P.O. Box 14,000
    Air Canada Center
    St. Laurent, Quebec H4Y 1H4
    Canada

Canadian Airlines International
    700 Second Street SW, Suite 2800
    Calgary, Alberta T2P 2W2
    Canada

Canadian Air Line Pilots Association
    1300 Steles Avenue E
    Brampton, Ontario L6T 1A2
    Canada

AIR TRAFFIC CONTROLLERS

The U.S. Federal Aviation Administration was the employer of 23,000 *air traffic controllers* in 1992 and expected to have 2,200 more in 2005, due to increased air traffic. Most are stationed in the towers at major airports, at en route centers along established airways, or at flight service stations near large cities. Some work for the Department of Defense.

Heavy responsibility puts air traffic controllers under great stress, so anyone entering this kind of work should be prepared to cope with extremes of tension over long hours. Unlike other U.S. Civil Service employees, controllers may retire on pension after twenty to twenty-five years—a recognition of the strain they undergo. Their numbers are not increasing rapidly because technological advances are taking on part of their work.

Training and Employment

Applicants for American controller duties must be U.S. citizens, under thirty-one years old, have vision correctable to 20/20, and have clear, precise diction. They should be college graduates or have three years of progressively more responsible work experience demonstrating ability to learn and perform air controller duties. Candidates with both a degree and work experience will have an advantage. Competitive examinations are given in major American cities by the U.S. Office of Personnel Management.

Chosen applicants are given eleven to sixteen weeks of classroom and on-the-job training at the FAA Academy in Oklahoma City. They learn aircraft performance characteristics, aviation regulations, the airways system, and controller equipment. Intensive training in flight simulators is given. Full qualification as a controller takes three to six years. Every controller is given a physical examination once a year and a job performance review twice a year. Controllers can advance to *chief controller, regional controller,* and to administrative positions in the FAA.

Control towers never close down, so controllers must work frequent night shifts on a rotating basis. In addition to their forty-hour work week, they may work extra hours for overtime pay or compensatory time off. The government gives them thirteen to twenty-six paid vacation days and thirteen days of sick leave annually; life and health insurance; and a starting salary of $22,700. Average pay is $53,800 per year. Extra cost-of-living allowances are paid for assignment in Alaska, Hawaii, or Puerto Rico. In 1989 the FAA started offering bonuses of 20 percent to induce flight controllers to work at airports in New York, Chicago, and other cities where job pressure is intense.

Controllers' salaries are determined by collective bargaining contracts. There were 21,000 controllers in 1976, and 29,000 in 1980. Then a long and bitter strike of controllers was ended when President Reagan dismissed 11,400 of them who were on strike. The number has grown slowly since then, and it's now back to 21,000. The trade union is the National Air Traffic Controllers Association.

Further information and application forms are available from the U.S. Office of Personnel Management, which also administers the written test. It's listed in telephone directories under "U.S. Government."

AVIATION SAFETY INSPECTORS

The Federal Aviation Administration (FAA) is responsible for the safety of almost every facet of aviation, including certification of aircraft, pilots, mechanics, and people involved in manufacturing aircraft. In 1990 United States aviation was serving 450 million passengers, a number expected to rise to a billion by 2005. There were 800,000 pilots and 500,000 other aviation personnel, along with hundreds of thousands of aircraft, all to be checked regularly by the FAA's inspectors.

To qualify one must have thorough experience as pilot of the largest passenger aircraft, as well as the smallest, with flight instructor and other certificates. Salary averages $59,300. Application and testing are through the U.S. Office of Personnel Management.

CHAPTER 3

CRUISE LINES

Passenger cruises have become so popular that many new ships have been built for the cruise trade—so many that the number of berths on these ships in 1984 was 50 percent higher than in 1981. About two-thirds of the world's cruise trade is generated in the North American market, but most cruise-ship officers are European, while most crew members are European, West Indian, or Asian.

There are few American cruise ships or freighters. The United States Merchant Marine has been in sad straits for years because of the cost of American labor, both for building ships and for staffing them. Costs are three or four times what shipowners in Europe and Asia pay. As a consequence, United States shipping has been surviving only when heavily subsidized by the government or when heavy defense spending for military or aid ventures brings employment to American ships. Congress in 1970 agreed to subsidize the construction of thirty new ships per year until 1980. This vigorous construction program was intended to revitalize American shipping, but in actual practice, older ships were retired or scrapped at the same rate new ones were built.

Many United States shipping companies register their ships in Panama, Liberia, and other countries in order to pay low taxes and avoid high labor rates. Americans can work on these ships, but at low rates of pay. Also, having worked on a ship flying a "flag of convenience," an American may have a difficult time later, getting a job on an American-flag ship, because a United States union might refuse membership.

Passenger transportation across the oceans has been taken over almost completely by the airlines, and the great passenger liners have been retired or adapted to the cruise trade. Cruising has been gaining rapidly in popularity and is the salvation of the passenger ship. Many new cruise ships were built in the 1980s, and about twenty were under construction in 1995. New York City, formerly the departure point for about one hundred cruises to the Caribbean every winter, built a new passenger ship terminal in 1974. Fly-cruise packages had been introduced, however, giving the passenger a flight to meet a ship in Miami or a Caribbean port; this gradually ended winter cruises from New York, but as more and more people discovered the delights of the cruise, the cruise season became a year-round industry in the Caribbean. From New York City, beginning in the mid-1980s, some 300 cruises departed annually during warm weather, sailing to Bermuda, the Bahamas, Canada, and all around the Caribbean. Cruises up the inland waterway to Alaska, and from West Coast ports to Mexico and Central and South America and the Caribbean are also increasing their sailings and bookings. Fly-cruise packages now also take North Americans to join their ships in the Mediterranean, in Hawaii, and in the Orient.

JOB OPPORTUNITIES

Careers at sea are still possible for Americans on American- or foreign-flag ships and even in the United States passenger trade. According to the Department of Labor, there were 54,000 water transportation workers in 1992. This figure includes 16,000 captains and pilots, 7,200 mates, 8,800 engineers, and 22,000 seamen and marine oilers. The total is expected to drop by 6,600 by 2005 because of intense foreign competition and new technology.

Shipboard work is divided among three departments. The *deck department* operates and navigates the ship, maintains the hull and deck equipment, and supervises loading, storing, and unloading of cargo. The *engine department* operates and maintains the propulsive machinery. The *steward's department* feeds the crew and passengers and cleans the living spaces.

It is possible to become *captain* of a ship with no formal education. The catch is that there are many Coast Guard examinations to take in order to qualify for the licenses that are necessary to advance. The person with no educational background is up against severe competition from graduates of the one federal and six state merchant marine academies.

To do it the hard way, one would obtain seaman's papers from the Coast Guard, wait in a union hiring hall until shipped out as an ordinary seaman, after a year take examinations to become an able seaman, after three years at sea take examinations for third mate, and at annual intervals, take examinations for second mate and master status. However, this progression would take many years, and even with master's papers, the seaman might not become captain of a ship.

A more likely path to advancement is attendance at the United States Merchant Marine Academy at Kings Point, New York. Like the service academies, entrance is by congressional appointment and College Entrance Board examinations. Students are paid a small allowance, and their education is free. The second year is spent at sea aboard an American commercial ship. Each graduate receives a bachelor of science degree, a license as third mate or third assistant engineer, and an ensign's commission in the United States Naval Reserve. Almost without exception, this is the course followed by prospective ship captains today. The law requires that graduates of the Merchant Marine Academy must serve at least five years in the merchant marine or the military.

The Merchant Marine Academy places nearly all its graduates in sea-going jobs before they graduate. Merchant marine officers' careers from that point depend upon their doing a good job, studying for examinations for second mate and master, and taking them as early as possible. After this, they simply must work and wait for a captain's job.

Engineer officers gradually work up to chief engineer. The six state academies are: California Maritime Academy at Vallejo; Maine Maritime Academy at Castine; Massachusetts Maritime Academy at Buzzards Bay; Texas Maritime Academy at Galveston; New York Maritime College at Fort Schuyler, New York City; and Great Lakes Maritime Academy at Traverse City, Michigan. All these schools charge tuition.

People in the steward's department generally work up from such unskilled jobs as mess attendant and utility hand to third cook, second cook (the ship's baker), and chief cook. Above the chief cook is the chief steward. The chief steward is not a ship's officer, but nevertheless is answerable only to the captain. On a passenger ship, the steward's department is by far the largest, employing many waiters and room stewards.

Opportunities for women exist on passenger ships, as stenographers, typists, and secretaries; as hostesses; as beauticians and manicurists; as cashiers and pursers; and as cruise or recreation or health club directors. Women are also employed as registered nurses or doctors aboard large passenger ships. Technical and administrative positions are expected to open up more, as the precedents set by the United States Navy are followed by the merchant marine.

WAGE SCALES

Shipboard personnel receive free room and board, so they are able to save most of their earnings, if they can withstand the temptations of the ports they visit. Premium rates are paid for overtime. Officers generally can earn about 50 percent above base pay for overtime and extra responsibilities. There are numerous strong unions covering most seafaring jobs.

According to the Department of Labor, water transportation workers averaged between $650 and $1,150 a week in 1992. Captains and mates had median weekly earnings of $871 in 1992. Median weekly earnings for seamen were $512. Captains and harbor pilots earned the highest salaries.

Further information is available from the following agency:

Office of Maritime Labor and Training
    Maritime Administration
    U.S. Department of Transportation
    400 Seventh Street SW
    Washington, DC 20590

Information on job openings, wage scales, and employment prospects may be obtained from the nearest union office or from the applicable union's headquarters:

Marine Engineers' Beneficial Association/
    National Maritime Union of America
    30 Montgomery Street
    Jersey City, NJ 07302

Seafarers' International Union of North America
    5201 Auth Way
    Camp Springs, MD 20746

International Organization of Masters, Mates, & Pilots
    700 Maritime Boulevard
    Linthicum Heights, MD 21090

Canadian Merchant Service Guild
  1150 Morrison Drive
  Ottawa, Ontario K2H 8S9
  Canada

CHAPTER 4

RAILROADS

Following World War II, the airlines gradually took over most of the long-haul domestic passenger traffic that traditionally had belonged to the railroads. Service on many lines became so poor that it seemed the railroads were trying to get rid of passengers. As new population centers developed, there were many places not served by rail, and no new rail lines were laid. Intercity bus service improved and carried most of those passengers who did not fly or use their own cars.

By 1970, railroads were accounting for only 1 percent of intercity passenger miles. In order to preserve some rail service, the federal government in 1971 created Amtrak, the National Railroad Passenger Corporation. ("Amtrak" is a contraction of "American track.") Amtrak started operating with only 150 intercity trains, a far cry from the 20,000 in service in 1929.

Amtrak was started just in time. It finally had been admitted that automobiles were a prime cause of air pollution and that individual transportation would have to be reduced by improving mass transportation, which causes less pollution. Then came the energy crisis of the winter of 1973–74, reinforced in the spring of 1979, which jolted Americans into the realization that a really severe shortage of gasoline could force the use of mass transit.

There were many growing pains, as Amtrak strove to meet rapidly increasing demands. New types of trains were designed and built, many cars were bought, and a nationwide computerized ticketing and reservation system was installed and operating in 1974. Many of the roadbeds were in poor repair, and introduction of high-speed trains was pointless until the roadbeds were improved. Amtrak improved the New York–Washington tracks so that fast Metroliners could travel at 110 miles per hour; they planned similar improvement on twelve other main routes. Stations, equipment, repair facilities, and maintenance shops belonging to the original railroads are still being gradually taken over and upgraded by Amtrak.

The Department of Labor noted 531,000 railroaders working in 1976, and only 433,000 in 1982. Railroad jobs were expected to continue declining at a rate of 1.8 percent a year, and they did. There were 116,000 railroad workers in 1992, with an expected reduction of 4,600 jobs by 2005.

From the point of view of the person considering a career with a railroad, it is important to note that Amtrak gradually is taking over more and more employees from the original railroads and adding them to its own payroll. Only a small fraction of all the people working for the railroads in the United States work for Amtrak; many more work for railroad freight companies. In this chapter, we discuss only jobs on the trains or working with passengers—the travel jobs of railroading.

Amtrak has been very heavily subsidized by congressional appropriations since its inception. Reductions in the number of trains operating, as money-losing service was curtailed, resulted in many experienced railroaders being unemployed or working in other jobs and waiting to return to railroading. This makes it difficult for inexperienced people to obtain jobs. Many of the currently existing jobs are carefully governed by union seniority regulations.

Canada's rail history has been similar to that of the United States, with passengers leaving the railroads to drive their own cars and equipment and tracks sinking into poor condition. Equipment and maintenance improvements have been made, but at high cost. The Canadian government contributed $597 million for 1983 expenses in excess of revenue.

Via Rail Canada, Inc. (VIA) is a federal Crown Corporation that manages Canada's passenger rail traffic. It provided coast-to-coast service using 11,400 miles of track and serving 750 stations: 140 trains a day carried an average 18,500 passengers daily. VIA had 3,500 employees, but had to shut down its long-haul operations in 1990.

RESERVATION AND INFORMATION CLERKS

Amtrak's nationwide computerized reservation system is an innovation in passenger railroading. *Reservation* and *information clerks* work around the clock to give schedule and fare information and take reservations for Amtrak trains. These clerks work with telephones, computer-readout consoles, and computer terminals at five major locations: Bensalem, Pennsylvania; New York City; Chicago; Los Angeles; and Jacksonville, Florida. Additionally, clerks at central-city ticket offices and at railroad stations can consult computer-readout consoles and quickly enter reservations into the computer. Toll-free telephone numbers connect the general public with the clerks at the reservation centers, who can handle hundreds of thousands of calls each day. In Amtrak reservation bureaus in 1990, the entry pay rate for clerks was $68.32 per day, or 75 percent of the base rate of $91.04.

CONDUCTORS

The conductor is in charge of the train, whether it carries freight or passengers. He or she signals the engineer when to start, and can order a stop for any emergency. *Passenger-train conductors* collect tickets and money and furnish schedule and fare information. *Freight-car conductors* maintain records of the freight in each car and its destination, and make sure that cars are dropped off or added to the train as their cargo dictates.

Conductors are usually male and are promoted from the job of *brake operator,* which used to be called *brakeman* or *trainman.* Passenger-service brake operators attend to car lighting and temperature and may help collect tickets. Many women are now passenger-service brake operators, and many of these will become conductors. There were 60,000 brake operators in 1982, a figure that dropped to 35,000 by 1992, but the 27,000 conductors in 1982 increased to 29,100 by 1992. Conductors, brake operators, and all train-crew personnel often work irregular hours, including nights and weekends—getting premium pay for overtime. Most brake operators and conductors belong to the United Transportation Union. In 1991, Amtrak conductors averaged $57,900 a year.

ENGINEERS AND BRAKE OPERATORS

Locomotive engineers drive great machines powered by diesel engines or electricity. In 1992 there were 19,000 locomotive engineers and 35,000 brake operators. Locomotive engineers earned an average of $59,600 in passenger service and $59,600 in freight service. Brake operators earned an average of $30,000. A few people are hired specifically for training to become engineers, but most are promoted from brake operator positions after examinations. Newly hired brake operators should be between the ages of twenty-one and thirty-five, with a high school education and excellent hearing, eyesight, color vision, and hand-eye coordination.

The new brake operator is trained on the job by the engineers with whom he or she rides and is given a regular assignment when one is available. Within a year of being hired, the helper starts an engineer training course of six months, composed of both formal instruction and on-the-job training. He or she must pass numerous tests to qualify as an engineer, then may have to wait several years until there is a vacancy. Brake operators in passenger service in 1991 earned starting pay averaging $21,700. In passenger service, brake operators are often called assistant conductors.

Most engineers and some helpers belong to the Brotherhood of Locomotive Engineers. Some engineers and many helpers are members of the United Transportation Union. Shift work is common in over-the-road work and in local lines and yards.

STATION AGENTS

Station agents in small stations sell tickets, check baggage, compute express and freight charges, and may direct the operation of some trains. In progressively larger stations, the station agent is a supervisor of these activities or an administrator of a large staff. Station agents usually are promoted from the ranks of railroad clerks, telegraphers, telephoners, and tower operators. Those in the last three groups direct the movement of trains from towers in terminals and yards. To be hired, they should be high school graduates and have excellent hearing, eyesight, color vision, and diction.

CLERKS

Clerks are the largest group of railroad employees. They work in railroad stations, company offices, yards, terminals, and freight houses. Most railroads require a high school education and may require applicants to take a clerical aptitude test. Some clerical training or experience also is beneficial. Most clerks belong to the Transportation Communications International Union. In 1990 their earnings averaged approximately $70.25 per day.

Railroad clerks can advance in many directions—to cashier, executive secretary, accountant, statistician, chief clerk, auditor, ticket agent, station agent, buyer, or supervisor. Both men and women have found opportunities in this area.

EMPLOYMENT BENEFITS

Amtrak wants its employees to advance and has a program to provide educational assistance for employees who want to take job-related courses of study. There is also a very liberal pass policy at Amtrak and on most nonpassenger railroad lines. Amtrak employees have *unlimited* free transportation on a space-available basis, excluding certain special high-fare trains. Employees' spouses and dependents are given twelve free trips a year and as many more as they desire at half fare.

More information on salaries, job openings, and job specifications is available from any specific railroad for whom you may want to work or from any of the thirteen unions with which Amtrak has bargaining agreements. You may wish to write directly to any of the following:

Amtrak
    60 Massachusetts Avenue NE
    Washington, DC 20002

Association of American Railroads
  50 F Street NW
  Washington, DC 20001

VIA Rail Canada, Inc.
  2 Place Ville-Marie
  Montreal, Quebec H3B 2G6
  Canada

Canadian Railway Labour Association
  100 Metcalf Street
  Ottawa, Ontario K1P 5M1
  Canada

CHAPTER 5

BUS LINES

The United States has a magnificent infrastructure to support bus lines: 3,857,356 miles of public roads and streets, including 42,500 miles in the unparalleled Interstate Highway System.

What a change has taken place since stagecoaches on rudimentary trails were replaced by intercity buses! The first such bus route was established in Oregon, between Bend and Shaniko, in 1905. Early buses, without springs and riding on solid tires, were exceedingly uncomfortable and often broke down. Drivers had to be innovative mechanics, but even with their best efforts, a bus sometimes had to be towed home by a borrowed team of horses.

With today's miles of excellent roads, buses can go almost anywhere in the United States and southern Canada, including large areas not served by airlines or trains. If efforts are strengthened to reduce dependence on private cars in order to reduce both pollution of the air and fuel expenditure, the use of buses will increase.

The modern intercity bus provides not only transportation, but also large windows and sometimes an upper deck for viewing the scenery. Most also offer air-conditioning, rest rooms, and comfortable reclining seats, in addition to a high degree of reliability in meeting schedules and an exceedingly low accident rate. Buses used especially for sight-seeing may have kitchens like those on aircraft, and attendants who serve meals. They may also have tour guides who point out interesting sights in passing and lead the passengers when they disembark to visit a particular site. Thus, buses are an important segment of the travel scene and will be growing even more important.

Deregulation of the bus industry in the early 1980s spawned 1,500 new bus companies, many of them small but determined to succeed. This brought the total number of companies to around 3,000. There are more than 40,000 intercity buses in the United States and 6,000 in Canada.

The majority of the American buses are controlled by the major nationwide intercity bus operator—Greyhound Lines, Inc. Greyhound Lines is a single corporation. It started in 1914 with a two-mile run for fifteen cents in an open seven-passenger car, from Hibbing to Alice, Minnesota. In 1987, Greyhound purchased Continental Trailways, its major competitor, and absorbed the Trailways system within its own.

Another major bus operator in the travel field is Gray Line Sight-Seeing Companies Associated, Inc., founded in 1910. In the United States, Gray Line has a total of more than 10,000 employees in its companies; about one-third of these are drivers.

Gray Line companies operate both long-distance and local sight-seeing tours. The drivers also serve as tour guides, so they have to be familiar with the sights on the route as well as being capable drivers. They also are expected to have good diction and a pleasant manner.

Of the total employees working for Gray Line, approximately 15 percent are reservation and information clerks, who are constantly in touch with the traveling public and travel agents by telephone or in person. Inquiries about jobs with a Gray Line company can be made to one of its numerous member companies around the world.

Deregulation of the airlines, occurring at about the same time as the bus line deregulation, had a profound effect on the long-haul bus business. Many new airlines sprang up, offering intercity flights at fares as low as bus fares. To make up for lost business, many bus companies that had offered only scheduled service began chartering buses to groups. Some began offering guided tours and package tours—in which the passenger pays in advance for bus transportation, food, lodging, and sight-seeing expenses, all at a package price. Greyhound has gone into the tours business quite heavily. The American Bus Association reported that 60 percent of all long-haul bus riders are on tours or chartered buses.

DRIVERS

Long-distance bus drivers start the day's assignment with a thorough check of their buses—brakes, steering, wipers and blades, lights, mirrors, fuel, oil, water, tire pressure and condition, fire extinguisher, first-aid kit, emergency reflector. They obtain tickets, change, and report forms as required.

Driving from the garage or terminal to the bus station's loading platform, the driver parks, then collects tickets or money as passengers board. Over a public address system, he or she announces the destination, time of arrival, and the stops en route. The driver regulates the lights and temperature and responds to any passenger requests. He or she also may load or supervise the loading of suitcases and express packages.

If possible, the driver repairs any malfunction occurring on the trip, such as changing a flat tire. On arrival at the destination, he or she makes out a report on the distance traveled, times of departure and arrival, fares collected, and any mechanical difficulties or accidents on the bus. The U.S. Department of Transportation requires the driver to keep a log of hours worked. Any fines incurred for speeding or reckless driving must be paid by the driver.

Employment and Training

The Department of Labor reports that in 1992 the number of intercity drivers was approximately 23,000, and average pay was $22,000 a year for new drivers typically working only six months a year, but over $48,000 for senior drivers working year-round. Salaries are computed on the basis of so many cents per mile driven, although an hourly rate is applied for short runs. Driving schedules average less than thirty-nine hours per week, ranging from six to ten hours per day, three to six days per week.

The U.S. Department of Transportation limits a day's driving to ten hours, which must be followed by eight hours off. The Department of Transportation has minimum age, health, and experience standards for intercity bus drivers, but company standards are generally higher.

Stability of temperament and emotions is important in this job, since drivers may be subjected to tension from driving long hours in traffic and from dealing with an occasional irate passenger. Continued courtesy to passengers under such conditions is difficult but important.

Newly hired drivers are schooled for two to thirteen weeks in company policies, federal, state, and local laws pertaining to vehicle operation, timetables, price schedules, recordkeeping, minor bus repair, safety, and driving. They are given written and driving examinations, and new drivers must have commercial driver's licenses. After that, they start driving on passenger routes under supervision.

Although completely qualified, past the probationary period, and fully approved by the company, the new driver may spend up to ten or twelve years as a substitute, filling in for drivers who are sick or on vacation, or taking extra runs, before being assigned to a regular route.

With seniority, the driver obtains more choice assignments, which are usually the best paying ones. A few drivers are promoted to become dispatchers, supervisors, or terminal managers.

Intercity bus drivers receive paid vacations, holidays off, expense allowances or accommodations for overnights away from home, and other benefits. The driver and spouse are both given free annual passes. The independence of the job is an advantage in the eyes of most drivers, along with the opportunitiy to deal directly with many people in many places. Bus driving requires weekend and holiday work.

More information is available from:

American Public Transit Association
    1201 New York Avenue NW, Suite 400
    Washington, DC 20005

Transport Workers Union of America
    80 West End Avenue, 6th Floor
    New York, NY 10023

Canadian Bus Association
    610 Alden Road
    Markham, Ontario L3R 9Z1
    Canada

CHAPTER 6

HOTELS, MOTELS, AND RESORTS

Throughout history, whenever it was safe to travel, there have been places of public accommodation. In Asia and Asia Minor today, there are small inns called *khans* that provide only shelter. The Bible mentions that the sons of Jacob, returning from Egypt, stopped at such an inn and fed their animals. It was a khan in Bethlehem where Joseph and Mary found no room and had to go to the stables, where Christ was born. Out on the roads, usually at wells, *caravanserais* were built at regular intervals. These can still be seen, particularly in Turkey. Caravanserais are huge stone forts, large enough to hold one or several caravans with all their animals and strong enough to defend them against attack by bandits.

Ancient Persians built luxurious inns along their fine road system, as did ancient Romans. When the Romans conquered Britain, they introduced the *taberna* for drinking and the *caupona* for overnight accommodations. During the Dark Ages, travel was possible only by groups that could defend themselves, like small armies. The Knights Hospitalers built many hospices for Crusaders and pilgrims to the Holy Land in the twelfth century, and in western Europe from this time on, abbeys often served as inns— some still do. In England there were about 6,000 inns along the highroads and coach routes in the 1500s. Caravanserais had been spaced about eight miles apart, and English inns were fifteen miles apart, showing that a day's journey now covered twice as much distance. The Industrial Revolution spawned railroads, and the resulting increase in travel caused construction of large city hotels. Spa resorts soon followed.

The first known hotel in North America was the Jamestown Inn, built the year the colonists arrived in Virginia, 1607. A postal service commenced in 1710, after which inns multiplied along the post roads. Resort hotels began opening at eastern United States health spas in the 1700s and on the seashore in the 1800s. Large hotels were built around city railroad stations, and as pioneers pushed westward, a hotel was often the first building in a new settlement.

The automobile caused construction of the first "tourist cabins" that later developed into motels. Travel increased with automobiles, and later with aircraft, and hotels proliferated around the world. Several international airlines built hotels in distant, exotic places in order to provide lodging for their passengers.

In 1995 the travel industry directly employed 6.3 million Americans, according to the Travel Industry Association of America. It generates $78 billion a year in wages and salaries.

Bricks and mortar provide only part of what the weary traveler wants—most of the remainder is service, which means people working to fill every request. Out of every dollar taken in by hotels and motels, thirty cents is spent for employees' wages and fringe benefits and the cost of their meals.

About 55 percent of the hotel employees in the United States are women. In past years, not many women were in the very top echelons of hotel management; however, more and more women have assumed positions of responsibility with major hotel companies. Recently, for example, Marlene A. Hetzel was sales manager for Hyatt International, a chain of forty-seven hotels around the world. Women have been in charge of public relations at the Kahala Hilton in Honolulu, the Pacific division of Americana Hotels, the Greenbrier in West Virginia, the Inter-Continental Hotels chain, North American operations of Club Méditerranée, Pick Hotels, the St. Francis in San Francisco, Commonwealth Holiday Inns of Canada, Island Holidays Resorts in Hawaii, Inter-Island Resorts in Hawaii, the Olympic in Seattle, and at The Plaza in New York City. In addition, women in sales, purchasing, credit, and accounting are finding no bar to continuing advancement in the hotel industry, and some are becoming managers.

Hotel work has increasing opportunities for racial minorities in the upper echelons, too. The director of personnel at The Plaza for many years was a Black woman, and many hotels' housekeeping departments are headed by women. There are opportunities for many kinds of people in hotels. The new arrival from another country, who may have no education and be unable to speak English, can get a job as a dishwasher, busperson, maid, or cleaner. He or she can learn the language and the business, and work up to a more responsible position.

One such person, John Christoforon, was hired at The Plaza in New York when he arrived from Greece at age fifteen in 1913. He worked his way up from helper, managed the employee cafeteria from 1925 to 1968, then became head cafeteria attendant when a new cafeteria was built. In 1979 he retired, in his sixty-eighth year at The Plaza.

Advancement is likely to be faster and further for those who enter the hotel business with an education. There are usually openings at several different entry levels in hotels, with opportunities to advance in various parts of the business.

About 10 percent of United States hotels are *residential*—renting or leasing their rooms for long periods. The majority of motels and hotels are in the *transient* or *commercial* category. The number of *resort* hotels is growing rapidly as more people flock to them for vacations. Many resort hotels used to be open only one season each year. Employees might work in a resort in the Catskill Mountains north of New York in summer, and in a Florida hotel in winter. Now, however, northern summer hotels are using skiing and other sports to attract a winter clientele, and Florida hotels stay open all year, reducing their rates during the summer.

Many a hotel or motel worker advances by saving money until he or she can set up an independent business. In 1992 there were 99,000 hotel managers and assistant managers working for wages or salaries and an additional number of self-employed owners of motels and small hotels. The Bureau of Labor Statistics forecasts an additional 45,000 employed managers by 2005.

HOTEL AND MOTEL JOBS

Modern hotels offer much more than rooms and meals for travelers. The variety of services they provide adds to the number and types of hotel jobs. Besides guest rooms and restaurants, a hotel may have special bars or nightclubs; banquet facilities; meeting rooms with audiovisual and translation equipment; large ballrooms; sales exhibit rooms; swimming pools; marinas; golf courses; tennis courts; ski tows and lifts; travel agencies; beauty and barber shops; valet services; airline offices; theater ticket agencies; newsstands; gift shops; babysitting services; car, boat, and plane rentals; health clubs; stage and film theaters; gambling casinos; teleconference rooms; business offices; and any other facility or service that will add income.

A large hotel may have six major departments and some auxiliary ones. The *executive* department may include a general manager, resident manager, controllers or accountants, management trainees, and directors of sales, personnel, rooms, food and beverages, housekeeping, and public relations.

In the *front office* are mail clerks, room clerks, reservation clerks, and the front-office manager. The accounting department has auditors, bookkeepers, office-machine operators, cashiers, and other clerical workers.

The *housekeeping* department includes the housekeeper, housekeeper's assistants, heavy cleaning people, seamstresses, tailors, launderers, decorators, upholsterers, and others. Redcaps, valets, elevator operators, and doorpeople work under the superintendent of service in the *service* department.

The *restaurant* department has chefs, cooks of various grades and types, kitchen helpers, a steward and staff, pantrykeepers, storeroom employees, dishwashers, food servers, bartenders, buspeople, and other food and beverage service workers.

The *maintenance* department has stationary engineers to operate machinery for heating and air-conditioning guest rooms and public rooms, and for cooling large refrigerators. This department also employs electricians, plumbers, carpenters, painters, and locksmiths.

Front-Office Workers

Front-office clerks do much of the hotel's minute-by-minute business with guests. The room clerks rent rooms and greet guests, assign rooms, sell various services, open billing records for new guests, advise housekeepers of arrivals and departures, and keep reservations lists. When a room is assigned, the desk clerk turns the key over to a bellperson who takes the guest and her or his baggage to the room.

Reservation clerks receive reservations in person or by mail, fax, telephone, or teletype, and acknowledge them. They type out registration forms and advise room clerks of each day's list of arriving guests. A reservation clerk may also make reservations for guests at other hotels on their itinerary.

Mail and information clerks place mail, messages, and keys in guests' boxes and give these out when called for. They answer telephones and route incoming calls to the right rooms. They also may sell stamps and advise guests about transportation, attractions, and events.

Most of North America's elegant hotels now have a *concierge* sitting at a prominent desk in the lobby. This is often a personable young woman or man who speaks several languages. The functions of the concierge are many and varied—providing guests with all sorts of information; arranging reservations or tickets for dinner, the theater, airlines, tours, sports facilities or events; arranging introductions; lending umbrellas when it rains; and solving any guest room problem of heat, cold, humidity, plumbing, or other inconvenience. Symbol of the concierge is crossed keys on the lapels. The position and the term *concierge,* long common in Europe, became widespread in North American luxury hotels in the 1980s.

The *front-office manager* supervises all these functions, coordinates the actions of the front office with those of the housekeeper and others, schedules work shifts and assignments of clerks, inspects rooms periodically, and handles the many kinds of complaints and problems that can arise in a hotel. Most front offices never close, so if clerks fail to arrive, the manager must find substitutes or fill in for the absent clerk.

Cashiers keep track of guest charges, total them when a guest leaves, or at regular intervals, and accept payment. *Accountants* bill guests regularly, handle the hotel's payroll, and prepare regular profit-and-loss statements.

For the person who is ambitious for success in the hotel business, the front office is the place to learn all about hotels and to learn to cope with all the problems that can arise. Openings for beginners' clerical jobs in the front office are usually filled by inexperienced newcomers. Sometimes bellpeople, switchboard operators, or other employees who appear capable are promoted to such jobs.

EDUCATION AND TRAINING

Educational requirements for front-office jobs vary according to the type and size of hotel, its location, and its own standards. A high school education is desirable. Graduates of two- or four-year colleges often start as management trainees, rotating from one department to another, but obtaining major experience in the front office. Even better for such a career is graduation from a two- or four-year course in hotel and motel management. These specialized curricula are becoming widespread as colleges realize the growing importance of the lodging industry. (See Appendix B for a listing of United States and Canadian schools in hotel and motel administration.)

It is still possible for a person without a high school education, but with good personality and native ability and intelligence, to rise to the top in the lodging business. Such advancement becomes more difficult, however, as college-trained people enter the business as management trainees. So it makes sense to obtain the best education you can. In addition to more rapid advancement, the person with greater education is generally paid more in top-management positions.

If you want to enter the lodging business directly after high school, try to attend a technical high school offering hotel-related courses. Courses that might be beneficial include cooking, business administration, management, and economics.

For its employees who have little or no education, the hotel industry provides training courses. In New York City, for example, the Hotel Association, in cooperation with the Hotel and Motel Trades Council, AFL-CIO, operates its Industry Training Program. Free fifteen-week courses, combining classroom and on-the-job training, are given at various hours to accommodate people on different shifts. Courses include English, basic accounting, repairs and maintenance, food and beverage control, floor housekeeping, telephone switchboard operation, night auditing, business machine operation, typing, and front-office procedure. There are similar programs in many cities. Many hotel workers who started as maids or busboys have profited by these courses to become housekeepers, cashiers, auditors, and room clerks.

High schools in many cities have adult education programs with specific courses for hotel workers. Some large hotels and chains have their own in-house schools, combining formal classes with on-the-job training.

An industry educational program applicable to a variety of situations is that of the Educational Institute of the American Hotel & Motel Association. These courses can be taken by mail on an individual basis, in small groups without an instructor, in larger groups with instructors, or in cooperating colleges that teach Institute courses. Courses cover many topics, from the basics of sanitation and bookkeeping on up to marketing and hotel/motel property management. People can take single courses in a special-interest subject, such as food and beverage operations, or take ten courses and earn the institute's diploma. Beyond this, by taking five courses in advanced management, having five years of industry experience, and demonstrating service to the industry, a hotel worker can earn distinction as a certified hotel administrator.

EMPLOYMENT AND SALARIES

Employment at hotels, motels, and resorts has advantages and disadvantages. There is always room for advancement for the hard worker who is willing to study and learn. Work in the lodging industry offers variety. When a person reaches the top in a small operation, he or she can generally move to a larger one and keep advancing. A person with a good record can usually find work in any part of the traveled world, and certainly in any part of the United States or Canada. Hotel workers in a chain usually can vacation in the chain's various properties at a fraction of the regular fee.

Busperson and housekeeper wages are low, but job security is good, and meals and uniforms are often provided, so that the cost of living is reduced.

At the middle-management level, salaries are good compared to those in other industries, and at top management levels, the salaries can be very high. Hours worked per week are comparable with those in other industries, but many jobs must be performed at night, on Sundays, and on holidays, which can disrupt social or family life.

The median weekly earnings for bartenders in 1992, according to the Bureau of Labor Statistics, were $250, including tips. Waiters and waitresses earned median wages of $220. Tips accounted for a high percentage of their income, and waiters and waitresses who worked in busy, expensive restaurants or hotels had the highest incomes. Cooks earned median hourly wages of $6.57 in 1992, and assistant cooks had median hourly incomes of $6.00.

In 1993, salaries of *assistant hotel managers* averaged $34,500—in hotels with more than 350 rooms, $38,400; and in hotels with fewer than 150 rooms, $26,000. *Food and beverage managers* averaged $41,500. *General managers* averaged $59,100–$44,900 in hotels with fewer than 150 rooms, and over $86,700 in those with 350 or more rooms.

SOME THOUGHTS ABOUT THE HOTEL BUSINESS

Harry Mullikin was chairman of a major chain, Westin Hotels, based in Seattle, and is a past president of the American Hotel and

Motel Association. Westin Hotels was named in *The 100 Best Companies to Work for in America,* a book by Robert Levering, Milton Moskowitz, and Michael Katz. Their selection was based on interviews concentrating on pay, ambience, benefits, job security, and opportunities for advancement. Westin was rated among the top ten in "chances to move up."

Harry Mullikin assembled the following thoughts specifically for you—the reader who may be considering a career in the lodging industry:

> The hotel industry provides an exciting, challenging career opportunity for a number of reasons. The art of hotel management as a career is one of the most challenging in the business world. An underlying factor is that it is almost completely dependent upon "people taking care of people."
>
> A successful hotel is one in which the public enjoys the experience provided by the people working in the hotel. In almost no other career can an individual meet, talk with, service, solve problems for, and provide hospitality to so many travelers. Ours is a "people" business. People make the difference between superior hotels and mediocre ones.
>
> As a supervisor or department manager in a hotel, the greatest challenge is to motivate the employees to react with genuine concern, friendliness and professionalism to the guests who provide our employment. For example; to get a hotel laundry worker to fold the hand towels correctly, and to want to do it well, is a rewarding task. Employees want to do a good job, and they need to be encouraged to do so. Developing people to this fullest potential is completely satisfying. If you could do everything in a hotel yourself, it would always be just the way you wanted it. The fact that you can't, and have to trust others to deal with your guests, provides the real interest in a career in the hotel industry. The goal is to satisfy the guest. The means is by working with and through people to reach that goal.

Another important factor of interest in a career in the hospitality industry is that there is no technical education required for success. I began my career as an elevator operator at the age of fourteen, and I now head a company with fifty-five hotels in fifteen countries around the world. Eddie Carlson rose to president, then chairman of the board, of United Airlines after starting business as a page boy in a hotel. Many of the hotel executives I know came through the ranks and obtained their positions in management because they could work with people.

In the hotel or motel business, everyone has a chance for a worthwhile life with both interest and challenge. No particular educational requirement is made for employment in a hotel, although there are some valuable courses offered which help. The quality most needed in a career in hospitality is the willingness to deal with people, both the guests and the employees.

For a different view on the same subject, New York University's School of Continuing Education proclaimed in mid-1995: "The hospitality and tourism industry is booming nationwide and leading the recovery in the New York area. Already the world's largest employer, it is expected to double in job size by the year 2005." NYU announced the beginning of new degree courses leading to bachelor of science in hotel and tourism management and master of science in hospitality and industry studies.

They say: "Hospitality industry leaders and professionals realize that the industry has emerged from the preprofessional period in which its most successful leaders came from the ranks. Today, executives and managers armed only with diligence and pragmatic experience can no longer compete effectively in a world dominated by institutional funding and sophisticated competitors." So get as much education as you can before you seek a hotel job.

Further information on hotel careers may be obtained from hotels near you and from the following list of national and international associations and unions.

American Hotel & Motel Association
    1201 New York Avenue NW
    Washington, DC 20005

The Educational Institute of the American Hotel & Motel Association
    P.O. Box 1240
    East Lansing, MI 48826

National Executive Housekeepers Association, Inc.
    1001 Eastwind Drive, Suite 301
    Westerville, OH 43081

Hotel Association of Canada, Inc.
    804–10080 Jasper Avenue
    Edmonton, Alberta T5J 1V9
    Canada

Hotel Employees and Restaurant Employees International Union
    1219 Twenty-eighth Street NW
    Washington, DC 20007

CHAPTER 7

TRAVEL AGENCIES

The travel agency business is growing. There were 32,497 agencies in late 1988 employing 105,000 agents, compared to only 7,867 agencies in 1970. Even in the recession years 1982 and 1983, the number of agencies increased by 9 and 10 percent, respectively. And despite the rapidly increasing number of agencies, the average agency suffered no loss of business because travel bookings and commissions increased at a faster pace than the number of agencies. Under these conditions, career expectations can be high. Travel agencies are deeply concerned, however, that their customers will start dealing directly with hotels and carriers via computer, bypassing the agencies. The Bureau of Labor Statistics forecasts an additional 82,000 travel agent jobs by the year 2005.

HISTORY

Ticket agencies have existed since ancient Rome, when postal employees sold tickets for the use of chariots and roads and made out an *itinerarium*—the ancestor of the modern traveler's itinerary. Operators of packet boats, stagecoaches, trams, railways, and steamships sold tickets in their offices for rides on their equipment.

The business of the general travel agency, selling tickets and tours on the facilities of other companies, was started in England by a printer, Thomas Cook. Railroads had just commenced operation, and Cook, an ardent nondrinker, wanted to use them to advance the temperance cause. In 1844, he chartered a train to carry people from Loughborough to Leicester, where they would attend a temperance convention and return. Charging twenty-five cents each, he crowded 541 people aboard this first special train, on the first round-trip ticket in history.

Cook operated other temperance tours that were very popular. He soon realized that people were more attracted by travel at low prices than by temperance, so he began operating tours for entertainment, education, and other purposes. Ten years after his first tour, 165,000 people used his transportation and lodging arrangements to visit a great fair at the Crystal Palace in London. Cook opened a London office in 1865, by which time he was already sending tours to Europe and the Holy Land. In 1866, he led the first escorted American pleasure tour, visiting New York, Washington, Richmond, Civil War battlefields, Mammoth Cave, Cincinnati, Niagara Falls, Toronto, and Montreal. In 1872, he led a tour of twenty-two people around the world. His son, John M. Cook, promoted the firm in America and other places outside Britain. In 1874, Cook introduced *circular* notes. In a slightly different form, these became known as *traveler's checks,* which now are issued by Cook's, American Express, and several of the major North American and European banks.

American Express, another major travel agency, was established in 1850 by merger of the firms of Henry Wells and William G. Fargo, who also organized Wells Fargo two years later. Initially, American Express was a shipping concern, but it moved into banking and tourist services and by 1918 was out of the freight business.

Cook's, American Express, and a number of other large agencies organize and operate their own tours, as well as selling tickets for all kinds of travel. They also make individual travel arrangements, and some agencies specialize in certain national destinations to which they send frequent charter tours. Others arrange trips for youth groups, ski enthusiasts, and other particular interest groups.

MODERN AGENCIES

Most travel agencies do not organize tours themselves. Rather, they are in the business of selling trips and tours offered by travel wholesalers and carriers. There are some 35,000 travel agency locations (including branches) in the United States. Some of these are operated by the owner alone; however, the average agency has five or six full-time and one or two part-time employees.

The *travel agent* gives out a tremendous amount of advice and information to prospective travelers, but makes no money unless he or she sells tickets and hotel reservations. Working for a travel agency, therefore, means selling; so a person not interested in selling should not enter the agency business. There are benefits to the travel agent's job—free or inexpensive "familiarization" trips by carriers and hotels, but the new employee is not likely to receive these. Low-cost air travel and hotel rooms are usually made available after a probationary period, but for the first few years, an agency employee might be able to use these only on her or his annual one- or two-week vacation.

Travel-agency employees need to be able to find specific information rapidly on all kinds of schedules, fares, special excursions, tour offerings, car rentals, guide services, seasonally varying hotel rates, and a host of other details. It usually takes many months for a new employee to become really useful in an agency, especially a small agency. In a vast concern like American Express, jobs are compartmentalized and easier to learn.

There are two women for every man in the travel agency business. Women own and control 45.8 percent of all United States agencies.

EDUCATION AND TRAINING

Qualification to work in a travel agency varies widely from one office to another, and some agencies will accept people with less than a high school education. All, however, prefer applicants who have completed high school. College training, of course, enables one to move up faster and further. Beginners often start as clerks, typists, stenographers, telephone operators, or office-machine operators. As they do the paperwork, they gradually learn about the business and can begin to answer inquiries and deal with the public.

For the student who hopes to enter a travel agency upon graduation from high school, valuable experience can be accumulated as a part-time employee working one or two hours per day, on Saturdays, or during summer vacations.

For the new employee in a travel agency, there are courses that help her or him learn the business much faster than would be possible by accumulated experience alone. The American Society of Travel Agents (ASTA) provides a fifteen-lesson correspondence course, the cost of which is reduced if the student is a member of or employed by a member of ASTA. The lesson topics are

- What is a Travel Agency?
- Travel and Geography (Eastern Hemisphere)
- Travel and Geography (Western Hemisphere)
- Domestic Air

- International Air
- Steamships
- Hotels
- Railroads and Motorcoaches
- Car Hire and Purchase
- Domestic Tours
- Foreign Tours
- Group Travel
- Documents and Other Services
- Selling

In addition to this course, handled by ASTA's national educational department, classroom courses on agency operations are held in major cities, typically meeting two hours a week for twelve weeks, for a total of sixty hours, in a local college or school. At many of these, graduates are awarded certificates.

ASTA also cooperates with companies such as TWA, Boeing, American Express, American Airlines, United Airlines, Inter-Continental Hotels, Westin Hotels, and others to provide courses and travel-agency manuals on many special facets of the business.

The Cruise Lines International Association, headquartered in New York, includes thirty-one shipping lines comprising 124 ships at the end of 1995. In 1993, CLIA introduced a major Cruise Counselor Certification Program, which provides advanced courses for travel agents that lead to an Accredited Cruise Counselor or Master Cruise Counselor designation. In late 1995, 14,000 travel agents were enrolled in the program and more than 3,000 had earned certification. For entry-level travel counselors, CLIA offers a classroom seminar in 200 communities per year in the United States and Canada entitled "Cruise Vacations: An Introduction."

ASTA's Washington headquarters also administers a course that concentrates on teaching travel agency personnel how to deal with the airlines and how to use their reference books, schedules, and computers. The course was developed by British Airways.

An industry-sponsored educational program of great importance in upgrading the professionalism of travel agents is the CTC (certified travel counselor) program of the nonprofit Institute of Certified Travel Agents (ICTA). To become a Certified Travel Counselor, the agent must have five years' agency experience, and complete a two-year graduate-level program, conducted in local evening study groups, which includes four four-hour examinations.

In 1983, ICTA launched a second course, the Travel Career Development Program, for agency employees who have worked in travel about a year and want to improve their skills and knowledge. This is a twenty-week course, also pursued through local study groups, led by graduate CTCs. Completing the course and passing a comprehensive examination earns the participant a certificate. A very comprehensive textbook, *Travel Career Development* (5th ed., by Patricia Gagnan and Karen Silva; Burr Ridge, IL: Richard D. Irwin, Publisher), developed for this course, is also used in courses elsewhere. A large-format book of 356 pages, it's highly useful as both a basic textbook and a reference book on the travel agency business.

JOB DUTIES

What does an employee of a travel agency do? Quite a variety of tasks. She or he—the majority of travel agency clerks are women—gives out travel literature about destinations, about airline and cruise "packages" that cover almost all costs for transportation and accommodations and meals, about bus tours in the local area, and perhaps about helicopter and train tours. The agent answers questions about comparative costs for accommodations and transportation as prospective travelers seek the least expensive or most luxurious vacations. She or he makes out itineraries that can be quite long and complicated if there are numerous stops and various hotels. When the client has approved a proposed itinerary, the *agency clerk* has to issue tickets and vouchers, sending copies to airlines and hotels to confirm reservations made by telephone, cable, fax, or mail.

One of the requirements for most agency jobs is typing ability because the agent has many forms to fill out. It is essential that these be legible. Advancing in the travel agency business, the clerk must write many letters about arrangements with carriers and about lodgings and other services.

Travel agency personnel sell traveler's checks and such special tickets as Eurailpasses; they also arrange for rental cars and escorted tours. By agreement with other travel agencies around the world, they can offer all kinds of local services in any city the traveler might reach.

Business in a travel agency changes from month to month, according to current attractions and time and money available to travelers. School and business vacations determine when many people take trips. The rich and the retired go south in winter, and the energetic go skiing. Resort areas have high seasons and low seasons and are always trying to extend the high season a little longer with special attractions. Atlantic City's "Miss America" contest was designed to add a week to the short summer season, for example, and it has been successful at this for eight decades. Many places have notable annual events, such as Carnival in Rio, Mardi Gras in New Orleans, New Year's Eve in New York's Times Square, and Oktoberfest in Bavaria. For the quadrennial Olympic Games, and for popular cruises, accommodations are booked in advance.

Requests to an agency are changing constantly, and clerks must remain alert to new tours, excursions, special fare offerings, and constantly changing fares and schedules.

A large part of the agent's business is arranging travel and accommodations for business travelers. This, in fact, constituted the greater part of the travel business until, in the 1970s, tourism became larger in gross billings than business travel. Some large corporations have their own in-house travel personnel to make direct bookings with carriers.

EMPLOYMENT AND SALARIES

How does one get a job in a travel agency? Jobs in classified advertisement sections of newspapers generally are listed under the "Travel" heading. Most such advertisements demand experience in an agency or in similar work for an airline or other carrier or hotel. A newcomer in the field should look for ads for "travel trainees" or for typists, secretaries, bookkeepers, file clerks, switchboard operators, or even messengers—anything to get inside an agency so you can start accumulating the necessary experience that helps qualify you for a better agency job.

The trade press of the travel industry also carries advertisements for positions. Among the publications you should check for help-wanted ads are: *TravelAge East, TravelAge West, TravelAge Mid-America, Travel Trade, Travel Agent, Travel Weekly, Business Travel News,* and *Tour & Travel News.* These circulate only to travel agencies, but an agency will probably give you a few copies if you ask.

Very large travel agencies may be approached directly any time because they must frequently hire trainees to replace other employees who have been promoted or moved.

In the nineties, corporate mergers of giant companies have occurred in the travel field as well as in most other industries. American Express purchased Thomas Cook Travel and is now called simply American Express Travel. Carlson Travel Network merged with Wagons-Lits Travel and is now called Carlson Wagons-Lits. IVI Travel merged with U.S. Travel System and is now called BTI Americas. These and Rosenbluth Travel are the top companies in business and corporate travel. The largest in the vacation and leisure field is Liberty Travel. Each of these companies has sales in the billions every year.

Travel jobs are handled by employment agencies, and there are a few travel-job specialists. The largest of these is called Yours in Travel. Jason King started it in New York in 1972, and in a few years had branch offices in several cities. Now he has branches overseas as well. He finds personnel for travel agencies, travel wholesalers, airlines, hotels, motels, resorts, and cruise lines in North America and abroad. The salary ranges he works with for travel agency personnel are from $14,000 a year for trainees up to $500,000 for travel-industry executives. He usually has more openings for experienced personnel than he can fill, and he's highly optimistic about the future for people in travel.

Computerization is firmly established throughout the travel industry, and it keeps advancing and changing. For example, the automated reservations system was called CRT for cathode ray tube, then it was changed to CRS for computer reservations system, and now it's GRS for global reservations system. The major U.S. GRS systems now are Sabre, Apollo, Worldspan, and System One. An agency usually rents or buys the equipment for one of these systems. A large agency might join two systems, to avoid the "reservation bias" that can be built into any single system. Familiarity with at least one of these systems, plus knowledge of personal computers and their operating systems, can increase your salary by thousands of dollars in a travel agency; by the same token, computer illiteracy can stop you dead.

Salaries in travel agencies tend to be good. In New York City, where salaries are higher than elsewhere in North America, the following were average 1995 salaries; entry level with no experience $14,000–$18,000; reservation agents with two years' experience $20,000–$27,000. In the leisure and vacation field, travel agents with two years' experience earned $23,000–$25,000; with five years $24,000–$27,000; with ten years $35,000–$45,000. In the more lucrative business and corporate travel field, travel agents with two years' experience earned $25,000–$32,000; with five years $32,000–$42,000; with ten years $45,000–$75,000. Some agencies, in both business and leisure travel, also offer commissions and other incentives above base pay.

The majority of full-time agents (78 percent) are paid a salary, 4 percent receive only commissions, and 18 percent receive salary plus commission. Among part-time employees, about half are on straight commission and about one-third are on salary, with the rest on salary plus commission. Salaries depend in part on the size, location, and amount of business in the agency.

Just as in any other job, there are certain disadvantages associated with working for a travel agency or being a travel agent. The business is seasonal, making it necessary for some employees to be laid off for a part of every year. Pleasure travel is considered a luxury by most people; therefore, it is often one of the first things to be cut from the family budget when there is an economic downturn. Agents can cope with a minor economic downturn by scheduling clients for relatively inexpensive forms of travel, but in a very serious recession, travel agencies may be forced out of business.

For employees just starting in the travel agency business, there is a great deal of detail work, which some people do not enjoy. Travel agents also deal with the public constantly, and a few travelers—

haughty, supercilious, and demanding—are very hard to please. At peak seasons, a travel agent often must work long hours and is constantly interrupted by clients.

Despite the best efforts of travel agents, travel arrangements can be upset by such unexpected distant events as a strike of airline flight attendants in Iceland or of airline mechanics in Paris, or an earthquake in Nicaragua or Greece. The agent then must work frantically to save as much as possible of an itinerary and replan the rest.

Because of the allure of travel, many young people are attracted to jobs in travel agencies. By the law of supply and demand, large supply means low price; therefore, beginning personnel are not well paid. For this reason, personal travel is considered to be part of a travel agency employee's pay.

Examine your reasons for wanting to be a travel agency employee or owner. If the main attraction is personal travel, rethink the matter thoroughly. Could you earn higher pay in another industry and perhaps travel just as much? You would be paying for your travel, of course, but as a paid passenger, you would experience no waiting for hours for space-available seats, nor would you be bumped at the last minute because one more ticket-holding passenger came aboard.

On the other hand, people who stick with an agency can advance to generous salaries, time off when *they* want it, and the pick of their travel desires over most of the world. A travel agent can sometimes please clients best by pleasing herself (or himself). F.C.M. Pauwels, a travel agent who operated the five-person Plaza Travel Service in New York, liked music and the Orient. So as part of his regular work he led groups of music lovers on three- or four-week tours of European music festivals, and also tours of the Orient.

SELF-EMPLOYMENT

Should you go into the travel-agency business yourself, as owner, owner-manager, or partner? If you have the capital, it is not difficult because agencies are always for sale as owners retire or decide to sell for other reasons. If you are not experienced in the travel-agency field, it would be much better to buy a partnership in a going business rather than buy a business outright and try to operate it from scratch.

What about the possibility of simply renting a store and putting up a sign to say that you're a travel agent? This probably would not work at all, since you would not be accredited to sell the tickets of the major carriers, and, therefore, would have to buy tickets through another agent and split the commissions.

Some travel agents have broken into the business in this way: working on a straight commission basis for a travel agency, they sell transportation and accommodations, splitting the fees with the agency. When they build up enough capital, know-how, and familiarity with the accrediting agencies, they go into business for themselves. Other people have done the same sort of thing, starting by chartering buses for church and club outings and selling tickets, just as Thomas Cook did at the beginning of his business, and gradually working up to becoming travel wholesalers. A comprehensive book on the subject is *How to Become a Spare Time Travel Agent,* by Stan Volin, who has been selling travel in addition to doing a nine-to-five job for years. The book may be purchased from Stan Volin, Box 571-Z, Hicksville, NY 11802.

To be an agent of any kind, you have to represent one or more principals. Travel agents represent mainly carriers and purveyors of lodging, food, and other services. Most hotels and tour operators are glad to accept any sale made by a travel agent, but the major carriers have strict rules about who can sell their tickets. They are grouped into several conferences, and each has its own rules as to financial stability, experience in the agency business, and personal responsibility.

A travel agency not approved by the conferences must obtain its tickets through another agency, splitting the commissions. When an established agency is sold, the new owner must qualify for appointment with each of the conferences.

The domestic airlines' conference is the Air Traffic Conference of America (ATC), 1709 New York Avenue NW, Washington, DC 20006. For international airlines, it's the International Air Transport Association (IATA), 1000 Sherbrooke Street West, Montreal, Quebec H3A 2R4. Steamship lines are under the Cruise Line International Association (CLIA), 500 Fifth Avenue, Suite 1407, New York, NY 10110. Almost all domestic rail passenger service is now in National Railroad Passenger Corporation (Amtrak), 60 Massachusetts Avenue NE, Washington, DC 20002.

Some 75 percent to 80 percent of all air travel, domestic and worldwide, is on tickets sold by travel agents, and the percentage for steamship travel is even higher. Lufthansa German Airlines reports that in the countries that provide it with the highest amount of revenue, 90 percent of tickets are sold by travel agents. This is the reason that so many travel advertisements, especially those of carriers, say, "See your travel agent."

In difficult times, when airlines are counting their pennies, they are apt to rely heavily on travel agencies. A senior vice-president of a major United States international airline said during a recent recession, "If a ticket office costs us more than to sell through an agency in that neighborhood, we close the office."

Commissions

Income for a travel agency consists very largely of commissions. On domestic air tickets, the commission is usually 10 percent, and 8 to 11 percent on international flights. On a package tour that includes both air fare and a week or so at a resort, it is usually 10 to 11 percent on domestic vacations and 11 to 13 percent on international trips. Ship fare pays the agent 10 percent for a cruise. Competition among shippers in the short-cruise business in the Caribbean has led to commissions up to 15 percent for groups booked out of ports in Florida, the Gulf of Mexico, and the Caribbean. Shore excursions from cruises pay 10 percent, and sight-seeing, entertainment, and tourist attractions pay 10 percent for individuals and more for groups. The commission is 10 percent on Amtrak rail fare as well as on long-distance or excursion bus fare. Auto rental pays 5 to 22 percent commission. Hotels and motels pay 10 percent for individuals and sometimes more for groups. Travel insurance against accidents, loss of baggage, missing a return trip, and so forth pays a commission of 25 to 40 percent.

Travel agents sometimes charge fees for such noncommissionable services as obtaining visas for a traveler, sending faxes and making long-distance telephone calls for last-minute reservations, and for working out especially complicated itineraries. If a carefully planned trip is canceled, an agent is likely to charge a planning fee.

A special type of travel wholesaler is the *tour consolidator,* who arranges the cheapest form of air travel—charter trips. There are usually no hotel or dining arrangements with such trips—only round-trip air transportation. The consolidator charters an airplane, or perhaps a block of seats, and sells transportation through advertisements or, more typically, to clubs or occupational groups that take care of the clerical work and collect the money for the trip. The work of the consolidator requires knowledge of airlines, a willingness to take risks, selling ability, and usually a fairly large amount of capital. One way to acquire the necessary skills is to work for a consolidator or in the charter department of an airline.

ASTA, primarily an association of travel agencies, is the major trade association for travel agents.

For further information about travel agency careers or courses, write to any of the following agencies:

American Society of Travel Agents
    1101 King Street, Suite 200
    Alexandria, VA 22314

Institute of Certified Travel Agents
    148 Linden Street
    Wellesley, MA 02181

ACTA—Alliance of Canadian Travel Associations
    1729 Bank Street
    Ottawa, Ontario K1V 7Z5
    Canada

Cruise Lines International Association
    500 Fifth Avenue, Suite 1407
    New York, NY 10110

Yours in Travel Personnel Agency, Inc.
    12 West Thirty-seventh Street
    New York, NY 10018

CHAPTER 8

PUBLIC RELATIONS

The travel industry must rely heavily on advertising and promotion to attract the crowds of travelers on whom it depends. Advertising, on the scale required to promote a Caribbean island, for example, is very expensive. When funds are scarce for advertising, the ingenious public relations professional fills the void by obtaining publicity through visits by travel writers and travel agents and celebrities, through celebrations and fairs and local events that merit press notice, and all manner of innovative activities that legitimately draw attention. Even with a generous advertising budget, all these activities remain important in continuing to attract travelers.

Persuasion through communication is the job of the public relations professional. More specifically, public relations for travel concerns the relations of corporations, governments, hotels, carriers, resorts, cities, and other organizations with their own employees, business travelers, pleasure travelers, and the public at large. Among the media used by public relations experts to influence people are newspapers, magazines, books, radio, television, speeches, photographs, advertisements, surveys, exhibitions, charts, receptions, and parties. Workers in public relations may serve inside the organization being publicized, or they may belong to an outside company specializing in public relations for one or many organizations.

HISTORY OF PUBLIC RELATIONS

From the most ancient times, rulers paid writers and song-smiths to create works that praised the ruler, inspired patriotism, and persuaded people of the worthiness of the current war. One of the functions of organized religion, also, has always been to support the secular ruler.

These were direct, naive public relations efforts, and there are thousands of similar examples throughout history. But the term *public relations* did not come into use until early in this century. Earlier, the Roman Catholic Church had instituted the word *propaganda* to describe its efforts to mold public opinion in the Counter-Reformation, and *press agents* were employed by both the North and the South in the Civil War to influence European public opinion. *Propaganda* became a dirty word eventually because people realized that much of it was false. The term *press agent* is seldom used now because of the work of press agents in covering up or glorifying nefarious schemes of the robber barons of United States industry in the late 1800s. The ridiculously excessive publicity stunts of press agents for Hollywood stars and other celebrities early in this century also added to their tainted image.

Public relations in its modern context started largely with Ivy L. Lee and Edward L. Bernays. Lee, hired in 1906 as publicity adviser to the Pennsylvania Railroad, began a policy of openness and frankness with reporters. For example, instead of trying to suppress press awareness of a terrible train wreck, he invited reporters to the scene and helped them to determine and report the cause of the accident.

Rather than just accepting orders to flaunt good news or suppress bad news, Lee and Bernays both gave advice to their clients. Bernays studied the people he was trying to influence and decided there were several different "publics" to be reached, and each had to be approached in the most effective way.

In 1927, John W. Hill, a newspaperman, opened a one-man public relations company in Cleveland, Ohio. His firm, Hill and Knowlton, became the largest public relations firm in the world, with offices in New York and seven other United States cities, as well as in ten European and Asian cities. Mr. Hill, who died in 1977, once said:

> Since the aim of public relations is to inform and convince, the good public relations person has a talent both for understanding and for telling. He enjoys explaining things to others and, like a good debater, wants to persuade. The public relations person thus tends to have an aptitude for expression. He is likely to be a good writer or speaker. Choosing the right word at the right time is of real importance to him, for he is sensitive to people's responses. The good public relations person has curiosity and thoroughness, too. To convince others, he must himself know; and to know, he has to dig. Thus the good public relations person has factual knowledge, but knows people, too—how and why they react, when and how to present his message. He must be concerned equally with the big problem and the small detail.

David Ogilvy, an advertising genius, emphasized the value of public relations in promoting tourism:

> Give your public relations budget priority over your advertising budget.... There is almost no limit to the amount of free publicity a country can get in newspapers, magazines, television and radio provided you don't starve your public relations people.... If I were running a national tourism office in the United States, I wouldn't spend a penny on advertising until I had spent $250,000 on public relations.

As the Public Relations Society points out:

Public relations, at its best, does not only tell an organization's "story" to its publics. The public relations practitioner also helps shape his organization and the way it performs.

OPPORTUNITIES FOR WOMEN AND MINORITIES

Rea W. Smith, formerly a partner in a public relations firm in Memphis, became administrative vice-president of the Public Relations Society of America, Inc., in New York, heading a large staff. She writes in *Business World:*

Historically, there has been less discrimination against women in public relations than in many other business fields. Women have been rising to the top rungs in public relations ever since the mid-1940s. The current head of public relations for Rockefeller Center in New York is a woman, and her predecessor, who retired after 20 years in the position, was also a woman. In addition, there are hundreds of women who own their own counseling firms.

And opportunities for minorities? Rea Smith continues:

The field has a crying need for black talent, not just for those people who can develop improved relationships with the black community, but also for those who can fulfill community relations and product publicity with all segments of the public, young and old.

The Society of American Travel Writers has 400 active members (writers, photographers, and broadcasters on staffs of publications or freelance); it also has 400 associate members who are all in public relations. Of these, 122 are women, many of whom head their own public relations firms and work for one or several travel accounts. Some head public relations divisions for states, major hotel chains, individual hotels and resorts, or airlines. Several represent national tourist offices of foreign governments in the United States. One of them, Jeanne Westphal, acted as director of the U.S. Travel Service, the government agency responsible for public relations worldwide to encourage travel in the United States. Women are building themselves an ever larger place in the field of public relations.

JOB DUTIES

There can be a great deal of variety in public relations work. The functions of the public relations agency or division can be broken down into eight specific kinds of work:

- Conducting research and evaluation
- Defining goals and planning public relations campaigns
- Building working relationships
- Writing and editing
- Disseminating information
- Producing communications
- Developing special events
- Public speaking

Conducting research and evaluation involves gathering the available facts necessary to a firmly based public relations effort, then narrowing the focus to those areas where changes can be effected. Library research, personal conversations, interviews with key people, and broad surveys of public opinion are some of the methods used in this process.

Defining goals of a public relations campaign avoids waste of effort and money. At this point, plans are made for the amount of money to be spent on each main part of the project and for particular people to be employed to get the message across to selected audiences. For example, a campaign to bring more tourists to Hawaii might entail sending a troupe of hula dancers and singers to perform at business luncheon meetings in the twenty-five largest United States cities, or sending some Hawaiian swimming champions to perform at swimming meets around the country. The cooperation of people outside the public relations office must be obtained well in advance, and they must understand their job as ambassadors with a message.

Building working relationships is essential in public relations. Much of the effectiveness of campaigns depends upon favors given and received, information provided on the basis of personal friendship, and newspaper space or broadcast time made available because an editor or broadcaster likes and trusts a public relations person. Within a company, a public relations worker must sometimes work through the personnel department, the legal department, or the marketing department, and her or his effectiveness is in direct ratio to personal acceptability.

Writing and editing form a major part of public relations work because print is the communications medium most often used. Among the writings of public relations people are press releases, brochures, pamphlets, booklets, annual reports, articles for trade magazines, statistics, survey results, technical data, newsletters, shareholder reports, employee publications—also film scripts, and speeches to be given by key personnel. Writing that is clear, lively, and effective in putting a message across will be an important part of any public relations work. As a matter of fact, many people who write well and want to be novelists eventually find themselves in public relations, where they are likely to be paid better (and more regularly) than they would be for writing novels.

Disseminating information to the appropriate editors of the relevant print and broadcast media is essential to communicating the messages of public relations to its publics. Keeping open the channels to these editors requires a knowledge of the editors' needs, schedules, and toleration and cooperation. People in public relations do their best to be known, liked, and trusted by editors.

Producing communications includes all the techniques of art, photography, layout, typography, printing, cinema, television, and other means of putting the message across. Public relations workers must work with specialists in these fields and must know enough about the techniques to see that they are used with utmost effectiveness.

Developing special events may take thousands of forms. A state tourist promotion director may invite a dozen writers on a tour of her or his state in hopes of getting them to write and sell favorable articles. A state such as Virginia may host a party for several hundred writers and editors in New York and show a promotional film to increase their interest in Virginia. An essay contest on local history may be held for high school students in order to obtain newspaper publicity for local historical shrines when the winners are awarded their prizes. News conferences, travel shows, ski shows, boat shows, camping shows, wild-water canoe races, and many kinds of demonstrations of equipment also are used to promote travel. Public relations people may do the original planning for these events, then obtain the cooperation of the principals who speak, compete, or otherwise earn the interest of the public. Finally, the public relations people prepare news stories and reports about the event, easing the way of reporters writing their own stories.

Public speaking is often important in public relations work. Often, a speech written by a public relations worker is delivered by a politician, company president, or celebrity whose presence makes the event newsworthy. A public relations worker needs to be an adept public speaker because he or she may often be asked to represent the client, company, or government by speaking at various types of meetings.

Public relations work is often frantic. If ghetto riots in a city cause prospective visitors to cancel reservations in the whole region, public relations workers must spread the word that areas outside the ghetto are not affected. An earthquake, a hurricane, a political coup, or an outbreak of disease can cause similar reactions and must be countered by public relations. Such crises may involve work, travel during personal time to the site of the difficulty, and statements from authorities to be quoted to the press. An airplane crash always gets headlines and inevitably causes a drop in bookings on the airline. Public relations people for the carrier have to work around the clock for weeks after a crash, trying to restore the reputation of the carrier in the minds of the traveling public.

Ideally, a public relations program is based on solid research, evaluation of facts, and determination of goals and schedules. Its various steps are planned for a period of a year to several years in advance.

Consider, for example, an island in the Caribbean or Mediterranean, for which a United States public relations agency is engaged to promote tourism. The island has only one hotel, small and very luxurious, but it has an ambitious construction program. In the first year, the agency might arrange visits by a number of celebrities to the one hotel, to build it up in the public mind as a "jet-set hideaway." As the island constructed the necessary infrastructure for development (water, sewage, and utility systems), the agency would report these items in the professional travel press, so travel agents would be reminded constantly of a new mass market to come. As new hotels were completed, the agency and the hotels would cooperate in holding highly publicized opening parties and celebrations and shortly thereafter would bring hundreds of travel agents on free or low-cost familiarization tours. Then package deals with airlines, hotels, and other services might be developed and publicized. Meanwhile, articles about the island's food would be sent to food editors; articles on crafts, history, sports, architecture, native habits, shows, and anything of news interest would go to other appropriate editors. The volume of news releases that can keep flooding out continually about even a little island is staggering.

This volume of press releases causes another problem. Every day, travel editors on metropolitan newspapers receive one or two mail bags full of publicity material. They cannot possibly print more than one percent of it, so the public relations writer has to use a lot of ingenuity to make releases and pictures distinctive enough to make an editor even look at them.

The Canadian Government Office of Tourism recently decided that it wanted to impress upon Canadians the importance of tourism. It launched an awareness/attitude program with the theme, "Tourism is important to all of us." J. A. Carman, manager of CGOT's publicity and promotion, developed a logo showing two hands clasped in the shape of a heart, against the background of a stylized maple leaf representing Canada's flag, with the slogan, "Reach out a friendly hand." Canada's tourism industry leaders were so impressed with this simple but strong invitation to hospitality that they decided it must be brought to the attention of students all across Canada.

EDUCATION AND OPPORTUNITIES

The young person aiming toward a professional career in public relations should consider graduation from college essential. Many of today's top people in the field arrived by way of journalism, and they consider a degree in journalism, plus a year or two of experience on a newspaper, the best preparation for the field. However, specific education for public relations has been expanding rapidly. In 1995, many hundreds of colleges and universities offered at least one course in public relations, and more than 200 colleges had degree programs or special curricula in which public relations was an important part of a student's course of study. Collegiate public relations curricula may be found in schools of journalism, communications, education, or business administration. Programs leading to a doctorate or a master's degree in public relations are now offered in more than sixty institutions.

The job prospects outlook for public relations workers is favorable because the industry keeps growing as businesses add public relations departments and independent agencies expand their activities. There were about 98,000 public relations workers in the United States in 1992. The U.S. Department of Labor expects jobs for public relations workers to increase by 21,000 by the year 2005.

Salaries in public relations fall into a very broad range. A survey by the College Placement Council found that new college graduates entering the public relations field were offered average beginning salaries of around $21,000 in 1993.

A 1992 salary survey by the *Public Relations Journal* also showed median entry salaries to be almost $21,000. Median annual salaries for all public relations account executives ranged from $28,000 in public relations firms to $36,000 in corporations. Annual median for all respondents was about $46,000.

Brochures on careers in public relations are available from the following organizations:

Public Relations Society of America
    33 Irving Place
    New York, NY 10003

PR News
    Phillips Business International
    7811 Montrose Road
    Potomac, MD 20854

PR Reporter
   Dudley House
   P.O. Box 600
   Exeter, NH 03883

Canadian Public Relations Society, Inc.
   220 Laurier Avenue, W.
   Ottawa, Ontario K1P 5Z9
   Canada

CHAPTER 9

RECREATION

Fitness has been a prime concern of North Americans and Europeans since the early 1980s. Hotels around the world now have running tracks and health clubs as standard facilities. Tennis, skiing, and other active sports attract more and more people. Increasing leisure time has led to the proliferation of resorts and sports areas and the growth of the National Park System, as well as state and local parks. In consequence, the demand for recreation leaders and administrators has grown tremendously during the past few decades. In 1972 there were 55,000 recreation workers in year-round jobs; nearly half of them were women. By 1980 the number of such jobs in the United States reached 1.4 million. The Canadian Parks/Recreation Association stated in 1984: "Recreation stands out as a career with a stable future."

Public and private support of recreation, although expanding rapidly now, is far from new. The stadium in ancient Greece, the amphitheater in Rome, public gardens, parks, zoos, swimming pools, baths, playgrounds, gymnasiums, opera houses, theaters, dance halls, athletic fields—all attest to people's inveterate devotion to recreation.

Since World War II, the number of hours in the average worker's week have been reduced, vacations have become longer, more holidays have been observed, and the moving of holidays to

Mondays or Fridays has increased holiday travel. In 1978 the U.S. National Park Service more than doubled the amount of land under its jurisdiction, to over 87 million acres in 314 parks. Many states also have set aside more land for parks, and commercial campgrounds have sprung up around many national and state parks to accommodate constantly overflowing crowds of campers. As a consequence of this growth, whole new industries have been established to manufacture recreation vehicles, houseboats, camping gear, snow skis and water skis, hang gliders, and dozens of other kinds of recreation equipment. New recreational villages have sprung up—second-home communities adjacent to ski areas, beaches, golf courses, tennis compounds, and primitive forests. All of these developments explain why the need for recreation workers is expanding so rapidly.

JOB DUTIES

What specific jobs do recreation workers perform? They teach dancing and lead social get-togethers to help people meet each other at resorts. They lead calisthenic sessions on beaches and in gymnasiums, aiding people in keeping fit or losing weight. They serve as lifeguards; swimming, tennis, and golf instructors; and coaches for all sorts of athletic teams. They also lead singing groups and impromptu bands and orchestras, and they enlist acting talent and put on plays or musical dramas at resorts.

Some recreation workers concentrate on activities with certain age groups; for instance, teaching skiing to children aged three years and up, or keeping senior citizens busy with checkers and other sedentary activities. Many recreation workers teach such handcrafts as leatherwork, beadwork, basket weaving, macrame, batik, sewing, crocheting, and model building.

Recreation workers can be divided into three major groups, according to their responsibilities. In the first group, consisting of camp counselors and recreation leaders, the work consists of *teaching people to do things* they can enjoy in their leisure time and *leading* them in sports and games.

The second group consists of *specialists* in particular activities. In a large camp for young people, one specialist might spend all of her or his time teaching people how to make things of leather, holding several classes each day. Another such specialist is the golf professional at a resort or country club. Recreation workers who have enough experience and enough capital sometimes start their own businesses such as camps, hobby shops, outfitters, trail-guide services, boat-rental services, whitewater rafting services, and craft instruction schools.

Above these two groups are members of the third group, the *supervisors and administrators* of recreation programs, summer camps, shipboard passenger activity programs, and the directors of city parks and recreation departments and of leisure programs for nonprofit organizations, corporations, institutions, and the armed services.

EDUCATION AND EMPLOYMENT

Employment conditions for recreation workers are usually very pleasant; they are helping people to enjoy life and to learn simple skills that give a feeling of accomplishment. Generally, a recreation worker should be an outgoing, gregarious person who is interested in other people and eager to help and to teach. The work should bring pleasure to the recreator, because he or she must work when most other people are at leisure—evenings, weekends, and the summer vacation months.

To obtain a year-round position in recreation, considerable experience is highly desirable, as is graduation from at least a two-year college and, preferably, a four-year one. The profession of directing recreation is a young one that is growing rapidly; as it grows, educational requirements will become more stringent. A person with foresight and determination will complete four years of college and go on to obtain a master's degree, and perhaps even a doctorate, in order to avoid being prevented from advancing later because of a lack of formal educational credentials. Many recreation workers specializing in music, drama, and art have graduate degrees.

Graduate work might well include courses such as business administration, since program directors must prepare budgets, allocate funds, and conduct their recreation programs in a businesslike fashion. Other graduate courses should concentrate mainly on the recreator's specific area of interest.

The Department of Labor says that median annual earnings of recreation workers who worked full time in 1992 were approximately $14,900. The middle 50 percent earned $10,700 to $19,900. The lowest 10 percent earned $7,700 or less, while the top 10 percent earned $27,200 or more. The American Camping Association said the average monthly salary for camp directors in 1993 was about $1,700. Recreation workers held 204,000 jobs in 1992, a figure expected to rise by 47,000 in 2005.

Hours of work average forty per week, but can rise far beyond that because of the irregularity of recreation workers' schedules.

For more information on careers in recreation, colleges with recreation curricula, and employment opportunities, write to one of these organizations:

National Recreation and Parks Association
  3101 Park Center Drive
  Alexandria, VA 22302

Canadian Parks/Recreation Association
  1600 James Naismith Drive
  Gloucester, Ontario K1B 5N4

American Camping Association
  Bradford Woods
  5000 State Road 67N
  Martinsville, IN 46151

American Association for Leisure & Recreation
  1900 Association Drive
  Reston, VA 22091

AMUSEMENT PARKS

Amusement parks in North America had sunk to a low ebb—notorious for their filthy food and atmosphere, pickpockets, confidence men, and dangerous, unsafe rides—when Walt Disney launched Disneyland in California in 1955. Disneyland revolutionized the industry. Everything was kept spic and span; blooming flowers and shrubs were everywhere. Most of the personnel in contact with the public were wholesome high school and college students, friendly and helpful. Engineering ingenuity was put to work to design new rides and other excitements and to improve old ones. All uniforms were clean, neat, and colorful. Something of particular interest was offered for all ages.

Employment at amusement parks is a two-tier affair. There is a small cadre of permanent staff and a huge horde of part-timers—more than 200,000 in North America in summer. The permanent crew includes executives in charge of maintenance, operations, sales, purchasing, advertising, public relations, food, and rides and their small full-time staffs.

A few parks in warm areas are open all year, but most, influenced by climate and school vacations, operate only in summer and on spring and fall weekends; all have cyclical busy and slow seasons.

In temporary workers, the parks tend to look for youth, wholesomeness, and outgoing personality. Education is helpful but not important. For permanent positions, however, knowledge counts—a degree in business administration, public relations, advertising, restaurant management, or food service (or perhaps hotel and restaurant management if the park owns a hotel) is an advantage. If you want a career in amusement parks, go after a college degree, and in your time off, gain valuable experience by working in several departments of various parks.

CHAPTER 10

TRAVEL WRITING

Making a living as a freelance travel writer in the mid-1990s is becoming increasingly difficult. Newspapers, whose Sunday travel sections had been the largest market for travel articles, are becoming fewer. As newspapers decline in number, however, all kinds of specialized magazines spring up. They do not use as many travel articles as the newspapers had, and their standards are often higher, but magazines of many kinds use travel articles in hopes of attracting travel advertising. This has increased the number of jobs for staff writers and editors. A growing threat to freelance travel writers is the decision by a few of the most prestigious magazines to refuse articles generated by sponsored trips, as a few top newspapers did two decades earlier.

HISTORY OF TRAVEL WRITING

In English slang a few generations ago, a "traveler's tale" meant a tall story—a highly colored and exaggerated account of adventures in exotic and faraway lands. Most of the world's literatures have included such reports. Homer's *Odyssey,* dating from about 850 B.C., not only relates the adventures of Odysseus (Ulysses) over the twenty years it took him to come home from the Tro-

111

jan War, but also describes accurately many parts of the Mediterranean world that he visited.

One of the world's most fascinating travel classics is *The Book of Marco Polo.* Fortunately for the world, this Venetian man of action, after his epochal journeys across Asia and his twenty-four years in the service of Kublai Khan, was taken prisoner in a war between Venice and Genoa. Using his carefully written travel notebooks, in 1298 he dictated to a fellow captive, the scribe Rustigielo of Pisa, the book that disclosed Cathay to Europe. Christopher Columbus had a copy of this book and made notations on more than seventy pages. His object, when he sailed in 1492, was to reach Marco Polo's Cathay.

Another monumental travel writer was Richard Hakluyt of England, who became archdeacon of Westminster and is buried in Westminster Abbey. Between 1582 and 1600 he wrote several books, chief of which is his *Principall Navigations, Voiages, and Discoveries of the English Nation,* describing all the great seaborne expeditions of English captains to America, the Arctic, the Pacific, and around the world.

If only some chronicler had joined the fishing expeditions of early Portuguese, French, English, and Scandinavian fishermen, we might know much more about ancient landings in North America. It is suspected that there was fishing from European ships on the Grand Banks off Newfoundland and Nova Scotia as long as a thousand years ago.

The first important analysis of the United States and its life is *De la democratie en Amerique (Democracy in America),* published in 1835, by Comte Alexis de Tocqueville. Sent to examine the United States penitentiary system for the French government, de Tocqueville wrote his report on prisons, and then, in *Democracy in America,* he described American life with such penetration as had never been applied before, and seldom since. He perceived that the great difference between Europe and America was the American insistence on equality, and he showed how this affected every facet of life, from emergent literature to science, religion, philosophy, the arts, language, business, the family, the military, and manners. He didn't care much for our ancestors' manners, but he foresaw that the influence of democracy would bring about the emancipation of women.

De Tocqueville's work would not be considered travel writing by some persons—those who believe that travel writing concerns itself solely with the traveler's transportation, accommodations, shopping, and recreation. But, in reality, this is the very best kind of travel writing because de Tocqueville delivers that most precious gift—insight.

The insight of the travel writer can bring the reader to feel kinship with people of another land and another race, by showing the universal emotions and motivations behind customs that seem strange, even bizarre. An alert travel writer is always attuned to the subtle emanations of a new place and its people. Every bit of feeling that a place arouses in a travel writer must be savored, perhaps analyzed, but certainly fully realized, so that the writer can express it in a way that makes the reader feel it as well.

Two men who strongly influenced the development of travel guidebooks as we know them today were John Murray of London and Karl Baedeker of Koblenz, Germany. John Murray (1808–1892) was the third of a distinguished line of publishers, all bearing the same name. He wrote a series of handbooks on the Netherlands, Belgium, France, the Rhine, South Germany, and Switzerland.

Karl Baedeker (1801–1859) started a printing plant in Koblenz in 1827. Under an arrangement with John Murray, he published a pocket-sized guidebook on the Rhine, Belgium, and the Netherlands in 1839. He subsequently brought out guides covering most of Europe and parts of North America and the Orient. These books were so reliable and thorough that the name Baedeker became a synonym for the word guidebook. The era of exaggerated "traveler's tales" had ended. Baedeker started the practice of marking with one or more stars in his books places of special interest or attraction, so travelers with little time could determine quickly what to see. "Starred in Baedeker" soon came to mean "well worth seeing." These *Baedekers* were published from the beginning in German, French, and English, and this helped them to gain extremely wide readership.

MODERN TRAVEL GUIDEBOOKS

In our own time, the mantle of Baedeker graced the shoulders of Eugene Fodor, a native Hungarian who became a United States citizen. He was editing travel books by 1936 and began publishing *Fodor's Guides* in Paris after World War II. He moved his headquarters to the United States in the 1960s and retired in the late 1970s. For each *Fodor Guide,* authorship is generally shared by a number of writers and researchers—whenever possible, experts residing in the country described by the book. Fodor has died, but the *Fodor's Guides* live on.

Quite different are the highly personal guidebooks exemplified by Myra Waldo's *Travel and Motoring Guide to Europe* and *Fielding's Travel Guide to Europe* (by Temple Fielding). These popular guidebooks, revised annually, depend for their attraction on the readers' confidence that they can rely upon the taste and preferences of Myra Waldo and the late Temple Fielding.

Arthur Frommer, after traveling through Europe with his wife, as inexpensively as possible, wrote *Europe on $5 a Day,* an inexpensive paperback book. The title's assertion that travel could be very inexpensive doubtless inspired many Americans to visit Europe. For millions of young people, it was a bible of essential information, carried around Europe until it was dogeared and tattered. It was such a success that Frommer started a publishing house and now keeps a number of authors busy writing and updating more than forty titles. Each book is written by a single writer or a team of two writers. Having achieved fame as a travel writer, then as a travel-book publisher, Frommer went on to become a package-tour operator and hotel impresario.

Many readers seek excitement, exotic scenes, and escapist literature that takes them out of their daily routines. Travel books do this, with descriptions of true adventure in jungle exploration or mountain climbing, treasure hunting or visiting natives of lost civilizations, archaeological exploration or sailing trips across an ocean on a raft. This kind of escapist nonfiction permits armchair travel and is at the opposite end of the spectrum of travel writing from the step-by-step Baedeker.

In between these opposites are many kinds of books on outdoor life, hunting and fishing, camping, ecology, folklore, local crafts, transportation, skiing, boating, history, cruising, flying, gliding, and so forth. Some of these are written to amaze or amuse the reader, others to give the reader practical advice and instruction.

As travel has become more widespread, the amount of travel coverage in magazines and newspapers has increased. Travel is a major interest, and people do more traveling every year. Another reason for the increase in the number of travel articles is that travel advertising has been increasing from year to year. A magazine or newspaper carrying a great deal of travel advertising must carry a commensurate amount of travel writing; otherwise, readers do not look at the advertising. If a Sunday newspaper's travel section had only advertisements, most people would discard it unread.

JOB OPPORTUNITIES

Although travel writing is important to readers, and therefore essential to magazines and newspapers, it is not a lucrative field for the writers. The reason is an ancient economic one, the law of supply and demand: so many people are willing to write articles on travel for little or nothing (and public relations people supply so many free articles and pictures) that a newspaper editor on a slim budget may decide to buy no articles at all, relying solely on free material.

During the economic slowdown of the mid-1970s, when newspapers suffered a shortage of newsprint (paper) and greatly increased costs (ink and labor), many newspapers that had been regular buyers of travel articles from freelancers completely stopped buying. They had their travel editors write articles, they used free articles from public relations sources, and they used articles provided by the wire services at very low cost. This is happening again in the mid-1990s.

FREELANCE TRAVEL WRITING

Travel writing on a full-time freelance basis is a highly insecure profession. As a result, there are very few full-time freelance *travel writers.* Many people who would like to be full-time freelance travel writers find it necessary to do some writing in public relations or in other fields in order to survive.

Staff positions as *travel editor* or assistant travel editor on a magazine or newspaper are much more secure. Almost never, however, is a person given such a position because he or she has trained for it or is a specialist in travel. On newspapers, unfortunately, the travel editorships are sometimes given to aging reporters coasting toward retirement, as a reward for past service. They get an opportunity to do some traveling and to write about it, but they do not regard such writing very seriously, and, consequently, readers are shortchanged.

To help combat such attitudes, the Society of American Travel Writers was founded in 1956. Its two primary goals are (1) to convince publishers that responsible travel reporting is an essential editorial service, an inescapable obligation to readers in this age of rising leisure and discretionary income and (2) to build joint strength of travel writers in support of their elemental function in the travel industry—as true spokespeople and travel critics for the average traveler.

The first president of the Society of American Travel Writers was Peter Celliers, who for several years was travel editor of both *Playboy* and *Modern Bride* at the same time—a piquant pair of markets. Celliers notes with distress that more than half of the United States newspapers and magazines that purport to cover travel do so without any professional consistency.

In 1980 a second national travel writers' organization was formed—the Travel Journalists Guild (TJG). Composed solely of freelance travel writers and travel photographers, its establishment was necessitated by the fact that freelance objectives could not be pursued in the SATW because they conflicted with the policies that travel editors in SATW had to enforce for their publishers. The founding president of TJG, Bern Keating, performed a signal service for all American freelance writers by obtaining the introduction in the Senate of a bill to amend the copyright law so that publishers would not be permitted to buy other than first serial rights of articles, unless other rights were paid for. The bill had a hearing but did not reach the Senate floor. Many other writers', photographers', and artists' groups joined ranks in support of the amendment, and the fight goes on. TJG had about seventy-five members in 1995. Membership is being kept small and highly professional.

Travel writing, for most freelance writers, does not earn enough to cover the costs of the necessary travel. Recognizing this (and hoping to obtain coverage of their attractions or facilities) airlines, resorts, hotels, railroads, cruise lines, and local and national governments often invite travel writers on press trips and cover part or all of their expenses.

In the early 1970s, several prestigious newspapers declared they would no longer buy travel articles based on "sponsored" trips. One editor went so far as to say this was a dishonest way of obtaining information for an article, despite the fact that his publication pays low rates, demands "magazine quality" articles, and pays no expenses. Under these conditions, of course, a travel writer specializing in faraway places must have other income in order to write for these papers. This cuts out the professional freelancer, in fact, and leaves this article market to those who do not depend on travel writing for their income—business travelers, pleasure travelers with a flair for writing, and others for whom travel writing is a sideline.

The same newspapers that reject press trips as unethical accept free tickets to plays, ballets, concerts, and sports events for their theater critics, dance critics, music critics, and sports writers. They also pay the expenses of any reporter who must travel to cover a story.

Writing about press trips, Richard Dunlop, author of numerous travel books and former president of the Society of American Travel Writers, said:

> I cannot imagine that any responsible public relations
> person who works for an honorable client, whether it be a

hotel company, airline, state, or foreign government, thinks he can buy a respected travel writer by inviting him on a press trip. Nor would a travel writer of stature go on such a trip if he thought he was being bought.

I have always felt free to write exactly what I thought of the areas I visited on press trips, and I believe that all travel writers who are members of the SATW should take the same attitude.

Another difficulty for people trying to become full-time professional freelance travel writers is that the "star" system is in effect at most of the best magazines. An editor wants to publish as many articles by celebrities as possible, so their names can be printed on the cover to help sell the magazine. This makes it difficult for a newcomer to break into the field and to sell enough articles to keep going.

This look at the problems shows that freelance travel writing is, in general, an insecure field. For those with talent and persistence, however, it is a fascinating way to earn a living.

TRAVEL EDITORS

A position as *travel editor* of a magazine or newspaper is much more secure than that of a freelancer. There is a regular salary, there are regular hours in the publication's offices, and, in the case of most metropolitan newspapers, a union contract to regulate working conditions. The Newspaper Guild, the union for reporters and editors, has been quite militant about obtaining good salaries and other benefits for its members.

Travel writing and travel editing are generally not recognized as specialties open to beginning reporters and editors in the newspaper world, so the neophyte must begin as a general reporter or copy editor. As more educational institutions develop curricula in

TTT (transportation, travel, and tourism), newspapers may begin to place TTT graduates in assignments that cover these subjects. Since the colleges with TTT generally do not require courses in writing, newspapers may obtain TTT specialists from among journalism graduates who have minored in TTT.

There are so few magazine travel editors that it is difficult to generalize about them, but it can be said that a college education is required for such work. Some travel editors are journalism graduates, but many are graduates in fine arts. For both newspapers and magazines, the master's degree is becoming increasingly necessary.

The work of a travel editor varies greatly from one publication to another. On some newspapers and magazines, the travel editor is actually the sole travel writer. Richard Joseph, for example, was travel editor of *Esquire* from 1946 until he died while on a trip in the late 1970s. He generally wrote two articles for each issue, and *Esquire* seldom bought any other travel articles.

On a metropolitan newspaper that buys ten to thirty travel articles each week, the travel editor's job is completely different. He or she generally works regular hours and is inundated with unsolicited articles, queries about prospective articles, and press releases from carriers, hotels, and attractions. Selecting articles, corresponding with travel writers, editing articles, and coping with problems of layout, photography, and deadlines require long hours, leaving the travel editor little time for personal travel.

On the prosperous newspapers, there are one to four assistant travel editors, so the travel section can be prepared even if two of them are traveling on assignment. On the papers with lower budgets, the travel editor may have no funds for personal travel or for buying articles. Then he or she must rely on public relations press releases and write an occasional vacation article.

To become any kind of a travel writer, editor, or broadcaster today, an undergraduate college education is essential, and graduate degrees help. A travel photographer does not need college training, but must have a great deal of technical expertise, as well as flair for the work. The competition in this work is very stiff—a magazine editor selecting photographs to illustrate an article often will have 100 to 200 or more offered, of which 1 to 5 may be used.

Further information about opportunities on newspapers and salaries for graduates of journalism schools, as well as a list of scholarships, fellowships, assistantships, and loans for journalism students, may be obtained from the following organization:

The Newspaper Fund, Inc.
  Box 300
  Princeton, NJ 08540

Current union wage scale information can be requested from the following addresses:

The Newspaper Guild
  8611 Second Avenue
  Silver Spring, MD 20910

Canadian Daily Newspaper Publishers Association
  321 Bloor Street, East
  Toronto, Ontario M4W 1E7
  Canada

Media Club of Canada
  (Formerly Women's Press Club)
  P.O. Box 504, Station B
  Ottawa, Ontario K1P 5P6
  Canada

Periodical Writers Association of Canada
  54 Wolseley Street
  Toronto, Ontario M5T 1A5
  Canada

OPPORTUNITIES FOR WOMEN

Opportunities for women in travel writing are good. The roster of the Society of American Travel Writers (SATW) includes about 40 percent women as active members. Active members include freelance writers, photographers, broadcasters, staff travel writers, photographers on newspapers and magazines, and travel editors in magazines, newspapers, and book-publishing houses. Women have presided over all of SATW's regional chapters, all of its major committees, and the national organization itself.

Opportunities for women in newspapers, magazines, and broadcasting are described in information from this address:

Women in Communications, Inc.
2101 Wilson Boulevard, Suite 417
Arlington, VA 22201

RECOMMENDED READING

Camenson, Blythe. *Travel: VGM's Career Portraits.* Lincolnwood, IL: VGM Career Horizons, 1995.

Casewit, Curtis. *How to Make Money from Travel Writing.* Magnolia, MA: Peter Smith, 1991.

Dun and Bradstreet. *Information Services: The Career Guide 1995.* Bethlehem, PA: Dun's Employment Services Directory, 1994.

Dunlop, Reginald. *Come Fly With Me! Your 90s Guide to Becoming a Flight Attendant.* Chicago: Maxamillian Publishing Co., 1993.

Farewell, Susan. *How to Make a Living as a Travel Writer.* New York: Paragon House, 1992.

Friedheim, Eric. *Travel Agents: From Caravans and Clippers to the Concorde.* New York: E. Friedheim, 1992.

Fry, Ronald W., ed. *Internships, Vol. 2: Newspapers, Magazine and Book Publishing.* Hawthorne, NJ: The Career Press, 1990.

Fry, Ronald W., ed. *Public Relations Career Directory.* Hawthorne, NJ: The Career Press, 1990.

Fry, Ronald W. *Travel and Hospitality Career Directory,* 2nd ed. Detroit: Visible Ink Press, 1992.

Gagnan, Patricia and Karen Silva. *Travel Career Development.* Burr Ridge, IL: Richard D. Irwin, 1992.

Garfinkel, Perry. *Travel Writing for Profit and Pleasure.* New York: Dutton, 1989.

Jensen, Clayne R. and Jay H. Naylor. *Opportunities in Recreation and Leisure Careers.* Lincolnwood, IL: NTC Publishing Group, 1990.

Krannick, Ronald and Caryl. *Jobs for People Who Love Travel: Opportunities at Home and Abroad.* Manassas Park, VA: Impact Publications, 1993.

Lesly, Philip, ed. *Lesly's Handbook of Public Relations,* 4th ed. Chicago: Probus Publishing Co., 1991.

Lovejoy's College Guide, annual.

Miller, Robert F. *Travel Careers Without College.* Kailua-Kona, HI: Gar Publishing Co., 1993.

Milne, Robert Scott. *Travelwriter Marketletter* (monthly). Waldorf-Astoria Hotel, Suite 1850, New York, NY 10022.

Mogel, Leonard. *Making it in Public Relations.* New York: Macmillan, 1993.

Morgan, Bradley J., ed. *Public Relations Career Directory.* Detroit: Gale Research, Inc., 1993.

O'Dwyer, J. R. Co. Inc. staff. *O'Dwyer's Directory of Public Relations Firms.* New York: J. R. O'Dwyer, published annually.

Plawin, Paul. *Careers for Travel Buffs and Other Restless Types.* Lincolnwood, IL: VGM Career Horizons, 1992.

Rudman, Jack. *Bus Driver.* Syosset, NY: National Learning Corp., 1991.

Rudman, Jack. *Bus Operator-Conductor.* Syosset, NY: National Learning Corp., 1991.

Seagle, Edward E., *et al. Internship in Recreation and Leisure Services.* State College, PA: Venture Pub., 1992.

Shaw, Eva. *Writing and Selling Magazine Articles.* New York: Paragon House.

U.S. Bureau of Labor Statistics. *Occupational Outlook Handbook.* Lincolnwood, IL: VGM Career Horizons. Published every 2 years.

VGM's Careers Encyclopedia, by the editors of VGM Career Horizons. Lincolnwood, IL, 1991.

Zink, Richard M. *Cruise Ships, Freighters, Tankers and Tugs: The New Employment Manual.* Dearborn, MI: Zinks Career Guide.

Zink, Richard M. *Cruise Ships, Riverboats, Casinos: The New Jobs Manual.* Dearborn, MI: Zinks Career Guide, 1993.

Zinsser, William. *They Went: The Art and Craft of Travel Writing.* HM Publishers, 1991.

Zobel, Louise Purwin. *Travel Writer's Handbook,* 2nd ed. Chicago: Surrey Books, 1992.

COLLEGES OFFERING DEGREES OR SEQUENCES IN THE FIELD OF TRAVEL

The travel industry has finally been recognized as one of the most important in North America. This realization, along with the industry's burgeoning demand for trained people, has caused a tripling since 1980 in the number of colleges offering degrees or sequences in travel-related fields. This growth is occurring so rapidly that it is possible to include only a selected list here. Additional lists are available from time to time in the annual publications *Lovejoy's College Guide* (New York: Monarch Press) and *Peterson's Four-Year Colleges* (Princeton, NJ: Peterson's Guides). *Peterson's* includes Canadian colleges.

HOTEL-MOTEL ADMINISTRATION

Alaska

University of Alaska
  Travel Industry Management
    Program
  Fairbanks 99775

Alberta

Northern Alberta Institute of
  Technology
  Edmonton T5G 2R1

Southern Alberta Institute of
Technology
Calgary T2M 0L4

British Columbia

B. C. Institute of Technology
Burnaby V5G 3H2

Camosun College
Victoria V8P 5J5

Malaspina College
Nanaimo V9R 5S5

California

California State Polytechnic
University
Hotel and Restaurant
Management
Pomona 91768

City College of San Francisco
Hotel and Restaurant Dept.
50 Phelan Ave.
San Francisco 94112

Monterey Peninsula College
School of Food/Lodging/Travel
Administration
980 Fremont Blvd.
Monterey 93940

Orange Coast College
2701 Fairview Rd.
Costa Mesa 92628

San Diego Mesa College
7250 Mesa College Dr.
San Diego 92111

Colorado

University of Denver
2301 South Gaylord
Denver 80208

Connecticut

Manchester Community College
Manchester 06040

University of New Haven
300 Orange Ave.
West Haven 06516

Florida

Broward Community College
225 E. Las Olas Blvd.
Fort Lauderdale 33301

Florida International University
School of Hotel, Food, and
Travel Services
Tamiami Trail
Miami 33199

Florida State University
Tallahassee 32306

Hillsborough Community College
P.O. Box 31127
Tampa 33631

Miami-Dade Community College
300 N.E. Second Ave.
Miami 33132

Palm Beach Community College
4200 Congress Ave.
Lake Worth 33461

St. Petersburg Junior College
St. Petersburg 33733

Valencia Community College
Orlando 32802

Georgia

Georgia State University
College of Public and Urban
Affairs
Hotel, Restaurant and Travel
Administration
Atlanta 30303

Hawaii

Kapiolani Community College
4303 Diamondhead Road
Honolulu 96816

University of Hawaii at Manoa
School of Travel Industry
Management
2404 Maile Way
Honolulu 96822

Indiana

Purdue University
West Lafayette 47907

University of Notre Dame
Hayes-Healy Travel
Management Program
College of Business Admin.
Notre Dame 46556

Iowa

Iowa State University of Science
and Technology
Ames 50011

Kentucky

Transylvania University
Hotel-Restaurant
Administration
300 N. Broadway
Lexington 40508

Louisiana

University of New Orleans
School of Hotel, Restaurant &
Tourism Admin.
New Orleans 70148

Manitoba

Red River Community College
Winnipeg R3H 0J9

Maryland

Community College of Baltimore
2901 Liberty Heights Ave.
Baltimore 21215

Montgomery College
51 Mannakee
Rockville 20850

Massachusetts

University of Massachusetts
Amherst 01003

Michigan

Educational Institute of the
American Hotel & Motel
Association (home study and
group study)
Michigan State University
East Lansing 48823

Michigan State University
School of Hotel, Restaurant,
and Institutional
Management
Eppley Center
East Lansing 48824

Schoolcraft College
18600 Haggerty Road
Livonia 48152

Minnesota

Southwest State University
Marshall 56258

University of Minnesota
Technical College
Crookston 56716

Mississippi

University of Southern Mississippi
Hotel & Restaurant Admin.
Hattiesburg 39406

Missouri

Crowder College
Neosho 64850

University of Missouri
Columbia 65211

Nebraska

Hastings College
Box 1204
Hastings 68902

Nevada

University of Nevada
College of Hotel Admin.
Las Vegas 89154

New Brunswick

New Brunswick Community
College
Moncton E1C 8H9

New Hampshire

University of New Hampshire
Durham 03824

New Jersey

Atlantic Community College
Mays Landing 08330

Middlesex County College
Edison 08818

New York

Cornell University
  School of Hotel Admin.
  Statler Hall
  Ithaca 14853

New York City Technical College
    (CUNY)
  300 Jay Street
  Brooklyn 11201

New York University
  Center for Hospitality,
    Tourism, & Travel
    Administration
  11 West 42nd St., Room 518
  New York 10036

Paul Smith's College
  Hotel and Resort Management
    Dept.
  Paul Smiths 12970

State University College of
    Technology
  Delhi 13753

Sullivan County Community
    College
  Loch Sheldrake 12759

North Carolina

Appalachian State University
  Box 200
  Boone 28608

Wilkes Community College
  Drawer 120
  Wilkesboro 28697

Nova Scotia

University College of Cape
    Breton—Tech Campus
  P.O. Box 5300
  Sydney B1P 6L2

Oklahoma

Oklahoma State University
  School of Hotel and Restaurant
    Administration
  Stillwater 74078

Ontario

Algonquin College of Applied
    Arts & Technology
  Nepean K2G 1V8

Canadore College of Applied Arts
    & Technology
  North Bay P1B 8K9

Centennial College of Applied
    Arts & Technology
  Scarborough M1K 5E9

Confederation College of Applied
    Arts & Technology
  Thunder Bay P7C 4W1

Fanshawe College of Applied Arts
    & Technology
  London N5W 5H1

George Brown College of Applied
    Arts & Technology
  Toronto M5T 2T9

Georgian College of Applied Arts
& Technology
Barrie L4M 3X9

Humber College of Applied Arts
& Technology
Etobicoke M9W 5L7

Loyalist College of Applied Arts
& Technology
Belleville K8N 5B9

Niagara College of Applied Arts &
Technology
Welland L3B 5S2

Northern College of Applied Arts
& Technology
South Porcupine P0N 1H0

Ryerson Polytechnic Institution
Toronto M5B 2K3

The Sault College of Applied Arts
& Technology
Sault Ste. Marie P6A 5L3

Sheridan College of Applied Arts
& Technology
Oakville L6H 2L1

University of Guelph
Guelph N1G 2W1

Oregon

Oregon State University
Hotel & Restaurant
Management Program
Corvallis 97331

Portland Community College
12000 S. W. 49th Avenue
Portland 97219

Pennsylvania

Luzerne County Community
College
Nanticoke 18634

Pennsylvania State University
University Park 16802

Prince Edward Island

Holland College
Charlottetown C1A 4Z1

Puerto Rico

Inter-American University of
Puerto Rico
San German 00683

Quebec

Concordia University
Montreal H3G 1M8

Rhode Island

Bryant College
Dept. of Hotel Admin. &
Institutional Management
Smithfield 02917

Johnson & Wales University
8 Abbott Park Place
Providence 02903

Saskatchewan

Kelsey Institute of Applied Arts &
    Technology
    Saskatoon S7K 3R5

South Carolina

University of South Carolina
    Columbia 29208

Texas

University of Houston
    Hilton School of Hotel and
        Restaurant Management
    4800 Calhoun Drive
    Houston 77004

Utah

Brigham Young University
    Marriott School of Management
    Provo 84602

Virgin Islands

University of the Virgin Islands
    P.O. Box 1826
    Charlotte Amalie
    St. Thomas 00802

Washington

Washington State University
    Hotel Admin. Dept.
    Pullman 99164

Wisconsin

Madison Area Technical College
    211 N. Carroll Street
    Madison 53704

University of Wisconsin—Stout
    Hotel and Restaurant
        Management Program
    Menomonie 54751

RECREATION LEADERSHIP

Alabama

Auburn University
    Auburn 36849

Jefferson State Community
        College
    Birmingham 35215

Lawson State Community College
    Birmingham 35221

Alberta

Red Deer College
    Red Deer T4N 5H5

University of Alberta
    Edmonton T6G 2M7

University of Lethbridge
    Lethbridge T1K 3M4

Arkansas

Arkansas Tech University
Russellville 72801

British Columbia

Selkirk College
Castlegar V1N 3J1

University of British Columbia
Vancouver V6T 1Z1

California

American River College
Sacramento 95841

Antelope Valley College
Lancaster 93536

California State University
Long Beach 90840

California State University
Sacramento 95819

Feather River College
Quincy 95971

Foothill College
Los Altos Hills 94022

Fresno City College
Fresno 93741

Fullerton College
Fullerton 92634

Glendale Community College
Glendale 91214

Golden West College
Huntington Beach 92647

Mira Costa College
Oceanside 92056

Monterey Peninsula College
Monterey 93940

San Diego Mesa College
San Diego 92111

Southwestern College
Chula Vista 92010

University of California
Davis 95616

University of the Pacific
Stockton 95211

Colorado

Mesa State College
Grand Junction 81502

University of Denver
Denver 80208

University of Northern Colorado
Greeley 80639

Connecticut

Northwestern Connecticut
Community-Technical
College
Winsted 06098

Florida

Florida Atlantic University
Boca Raton 33431

Florida State University
Tallahassee 32306

Miami-Dade Community College
Miami 33132

Palm Beach Community College
Lake Worth 33461

Georgia

DeKalb Technical Institute
Clarkston 30021

Georgia Southern University
Statesboro 30460

South Georgia College
Douglas 31533

University of Georgia
Athens 30602

Hawaii

University of Hawaii at Manoa
Honolulu 96822

Illinois

College of DuPage
Glen Ellyn 60137

Moraine Valley Community
College
Palos Hills 60465

Triton College
River Grove 60171

Indiana

Indiana University
Bloomington 47405

Kentucky

Ashland Community College
Ashland 41101

Hopkinsville Community College
Hopkinsville 42241

Louisiana

Northwestern State University
Natchitoches 71497

Manitoba

University of Manitoba
School of Physical Education
Winnipeg R3T 2N2

Maryland

Baltimore City Community
College
Baltimore 21215

Montgomery College, Rockville
Campus
Rockville 20850

University of Maryland
College Park 20742

Massachusetts

Berkshire Community College
Pittsfield 01201

Greenfield Community College
Greenfield 01301

Northeastern University
   Boston 02115

Springfield College
   Springfield 01109

Michigan

Eastern Michigan University
   Ypsilanti 48197

Michigan State University
   East Lansing 48824

Wayne State University
   Detroit 48202

Minnesota

Mankato State University
   Mankato 56002

Normandale Community College
   Bloomington 55431

North Hennepin Community
      College
   Minneapolis 55445

Missouri

Central Missouri State University
   Warrensburg 64093

Nebraska

University of Nebraska
   Omaha 68182

Nevada

University of Nevada
   Las Vegas 89154

Newfoundland

College of Trades & Technology
   St. John's A1C 5P7

New York

Columbia University
   New York 10027

Genesee Community College
   Batavia 14020

New York University
   New York 10011

Paul Smith's College of Arts &
      Science
   Paul Smiths 12970

State University of New York
      College at Cortland
   Cortland 13045

Syracuse University
   Syracuse 13244

North Carolina

University of North Carolina
   Greensboro 27412

Nova Scotia

Acadia University
  Wolfville B0P 1X0

Dalhousie University
  School of Physical Education
  Halifax B3H 3J5

Ohio

Kent State University
  Kent 44242

Ohio University
  Athens 45701

Oklahoma

University of Tulsa
  Tulsa 74104

Ontario

Centennial College of Applied
    Arts & Technology
  Scarborough M1K 5E9

Fanshawe College
  London N5W 5H1

Humber College of Applied Arts
    & Technology
  Etobicoke M9W 5L7

University of Ottawa
  Department of Recreology
  Ottawa K1N 6N5

University of Waterloo
  Waterloo N2L 3G1

Pennsylvania

California University of
    Pennsylvania
  California 15419

Pennsylvania State University
  University Park 16802

Saskatchewan

Kelsey Institute of Applied Arts &
    Sciences
  Saskatoon S7K 3R5

Texas

Tarrant County Jr. College South
    Campus
  Fort Worth 76102

Texas Woman's University
  Denton 76204

Utah

Brigham Young University
  Provo 84602

Vermont

Goddard College
  Plainfield 05667

Virginia

Radford University
  Radford 24142

Virginia Commonwealth
University
Richmond 23284

Washington

Bellevue Community College
Bellevue 98007

Big Bend Community College
Moses Lake 98837

Everett Community College
Everett 98201

Highline Community College
Des Moines 98198

University of Washington
Seattle 98195

West Virginia

West Virginia University
Morgantown 26506

Wisconsin

University of Wisconsin
Madison 53706

TOURISM AND TRAVEL MANAGEMENT

Alaska

University of Alaska
Travel Industry Management
Program
117 Bunnell
Fairbanks 99775

Alberta

Grant MacEwan Community
College
Edmonton T5J 3E4

Southern Alberta Institute of
Technology
Calgary T2M 0L4

British Columbia

B. C. Institute of Technology
Burnaby V5G 3H2

California

Los Angeles Trade-Technical
College
Los Angeles 90015

Mount San Antonio College
Walnut 91789

Colorado

Mesa State College
Grand Junction 81502

University of Denver
Denver 80208

Connecticut

University of New Haven
300 Orange Avenue
West Haven 06516

District of Columbia

The George Washington
University
Human Kinetics & Leisure
Studies
Washington 20052

Florida

Florida International University
School of Hotel, Food, and
Travel Services
Tamiami Trail
Miami 33177

Florida State University
Hotel and Restaurant Admin.
College of Business
Tallahassee 32306

Hawaii

Chaminade University of
Honolulu
Honolulu 96816

University of Hawaii at Manoa
School of Travel Industry
Management
Honolulu 96822

Illinois

Parks College of Aeronautical
Technology of St. Louis
University
Institute of Transportation,
Travel & Tourism
Cahokia 62206

Indiana

University of Notre Dame
Hayes-Healy Travel
Management Program
College of Business Admin.
Notre Dame 46556

Louisiana

University of New Orleans
School of Hotel, Restaurant &
Travel Admin.
New Orleans 70148

Michigan

Educational Institute of the
American Hotel & Motel
Association (for individual
and group study)
Michigan State University
School of Hotel, Restaurant,
and Institutional
Management
East Lansing 48823

Michigan State University
School of Hotel, Restaurant,
and Institutional
Management
East Lansing 48824

Nevada

University of Nevada
    College of Hotel Admin.
    Las Vegas 89154

New York

Adelphi University
    Transportation, Travel, and
        Tourism Program
    School of Business Admin.
    Garden City 11530

Genesee Community College
    Batavia 14020

Herkimer County Community
        College
    Herkimer 13350

New School for Social Research
    Graduate School of
        Management
    Dept. of Tourism and Travel
        Administration
    66 Fifth Avenue
    New York 10011

New York University
    School of Continuing Education
    25 West Fourth Street
    New York 10012

Niagara University
    Institute of Transportation,
        Travel, and Tourism
    Niagara University 14109

Paul Smith's College
    Hotel and Resort Management
        Dept.
    Paul Smiths 12970

Rochester Institute of Technology
    Dept. of Food Admin. & Tourist
        Industries Management
    1 Lomb Memorial Drive
    Rochester 14623

Ontario

Algonquin College of Applied
        Arts & Technology
    Nepean K2G 1V8

Centennial College of Applied
        Arts & Technology
    Scarborough M1K 5E9

The Confederation College of
        Applied Arts & Technology
    Thunder Bay P7C 4W1

Fanshawe College
    London N5W 5H1

Humber College of Applied Arts
        & Technology
    Etobicoke M9W 5L7

Niagara College of Applied Arts &
        Technology
    Welland L3B 5S2

Ryerson Polytechnic Institute
    Toronto M5B 2K3

Seneca College—King Campus
    R. R. No. 3, King City

Sheridan College of Applied Arts
        & Technology
    Oakville L6H 2L1

Sir Sandford Fleming College—
        Brealey Campus
    Peterborough K9J 7B1

Quebec

Concordia University
Montreal H3G 1M8

McGill University
Montreal H3A 3N6

Rhode Island

Johnson & Wales University
Providence 02903

TRANSPORTATION

Alabama

Auburn University
Auburn 36849

University of Alabama
Tuscaloosa 35487

Arizona

University of Arizona
Tucson 85721

California

Canada College
Redwood City 94061

College of San Mateo
San Mateo 94402

De Anza College
Cupertino 95014

Foothill College
Los Altos Hills 94022

Fresno City College
Fresno 93741

Golden Gate University
San Francisco 94105

Los Angeles City College
Los Angeles 90029

Los Angeles Trade-Technical
College
Los Angeles 90015

Merritt College
Oakland 94619

Mira Costa College
Oceanside 92056

San Bernadino Valley College
San Bernadino 92410

San Diego City College
San Diego 92107

San Francisco State University
San Francisco 94132

San Jose City College
San Jose 95128

Connecticut

Yale University
New Haven 06520

District of Columbia

American University
  Washington, DC 20016

Georgetown University
  Washington, DC 20057

Hawaii

University of Hawaii at Manoa
  Honolulu 96822

Illinois

Kennedy-King College, Chicago
    City College
    Chicago 60621

Lewis & Clark Community
    College
    Godfrey 62035

Moraine Valley Community
    College
    Palos Hills 60465

Parks College of Aeronautical
    Technology of St. Louis
    University
    Cahokia 62206

Prairie State College
    Chicago Heights 60411

Richard J. Daley College, Chicago
    City College
    Chicago 60652

Waubonsee Community College
    Sugar Grove 60554

Indiana

Tri-State University
  Angola 46703

University of Notre Dame
  Notre Dame 46556

Kentucky

University of Louisville
  Louisville 40292

Louisiana

Louisiana State University
  Baton Rouge 70803

Maryland

Essex Community College
  Baltimore County 21237

University of Baltimore
  Baltimore 21201

Michigan

Davenport College of Business
  Grand Rapids 49503

Michigan State University
  East Lansing 48824

Minnesota

Austin Community College
  Austin 55912

Mississippi

Mississippi State Unviersity
Mississippi State 39762

Missouri

University of Missouri
Kansas City 64110

New York

Adelphi University
Garden City 11530

Alfred University
Alfred 14802

Columbia University
New York 10027

Niagara University
Niagara University 14109

Polytechnic University
Brooklyn 11201

Queensborough Community
College of the City
University of New York
Bayside 11364

State University of New York
Maritime College
Throgs Neck 10465

Syracuse University
Syracuse 13244

U.S. Merchant Marine Academy
Kings Point 11024

North Carolina

University of North Carolina
Wilmington 28403

Ohio

Cuyahoga Community College
Cleveland 44115

Kent State University
Kent 44242

Ohio State University
Columbus 43210

University of Akron
Akron 44325

Ontario

The Confederation College of
Applied Arts & Technology
Thunder Bay P7C 4W1

Humber College of Applied Arts
& Technology
Etobicoke M9W 5L7

Seneca College—King Campus
R. R. No. 3, King City

Sir Sandford Fleming College
Peterborough K9J 7B1

Oregon

University of Oregon
Eugene 97403

Pennsylvania

Robert Morris College
   Coraopolis 15108

University of Pennsylvania
   Philadelphia 19104

Tennessee

East Tennessee State University
   Johnson City 37614

University of Tennessee
   Knoxville 37996

Virginia

University of Richmond
   Richmond 23173

Washington

Green River Community College
   Auburn 98002

Highline Community College
   Des Moines 98198

University of Washington
   Seattle 98195